Z O O
OF THE
G O D S

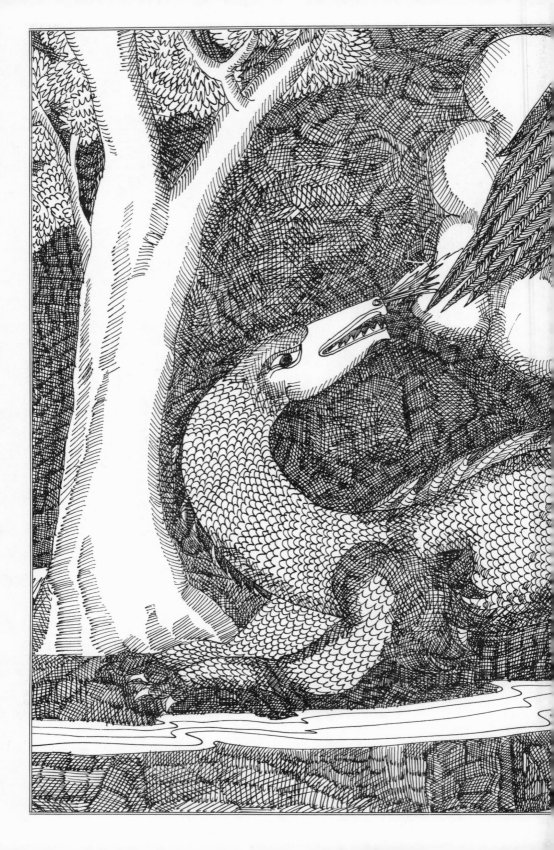

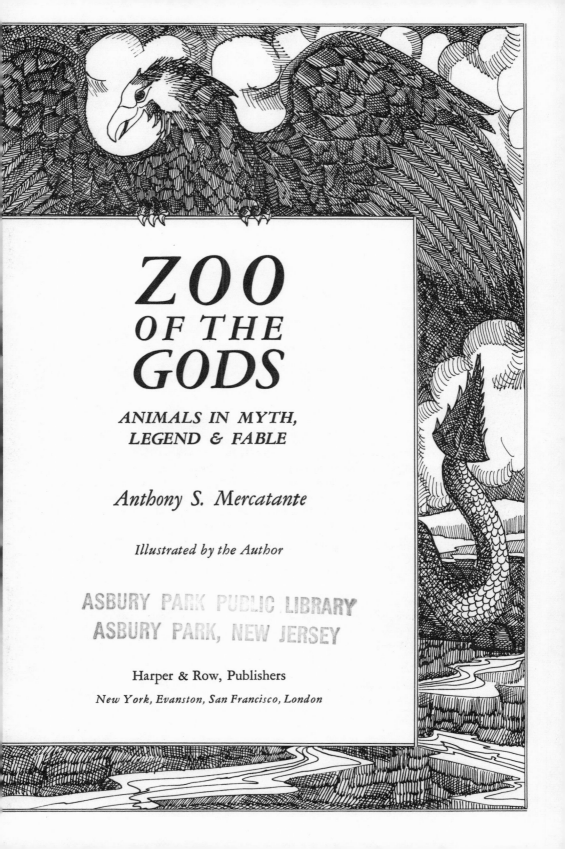

ZOO
OF THE
GODS

ANIMALS IN MYTH, LEGEND & FABLE

Anthony S. Mercatante

Illustrated by the Author

Harper & Row, Publishers
New York, Evanston, San Francisco, London

ZOO OF THE GODS: *Animals in Myth, Legend, and Fable.* Copyright © 1974 by Anthony S. Mercatante. All rights reserved. Printed in the United States of America. No part of this book may be used or reproduced in any manner whatsoever without written permission except in the case of brief quotations embodied in critical articles and reviews. For information address Harper & Row, Publishers, Inc., 10 East 53rd Street, New York, N.Y. 10022. Published simultaneously in Canada by Fitzhenry & Whiteside Limited, Toronto.

Library of Congress Cataloging in Publication Data

Mercatante, Anthony S
  Zoo of the gods.

  Bibliography: p.
  1. Animal lore. 2. Animals, Legends and stories of. 3. Animals, Mythical. I. Title.
GR705.M47   398'.369   74–4618
ISBN 0–06–065561–5

FIRST EDITION

Designed by Janice Willcocks Stern

For My Mother
and in
Memory of My Father

CONTENTS

ACKNOWLEDGMENTS

I wish to thank my editor Marie Cantlon for having suggested the idea for the book, and for her encouragement during the entire writing process. Next, J. B. Singer, who assisted with the research and with all other stages of the book, deserves my deep appreciation. Critical comments, encouragement, and advice were gratefully received from Kathleen Yerger Johnstone, Louis Untermeyer, Raphael Patai, Vine Deloria, Bergen Evans, Salvatore Iacone, Jean-Louis d'Heilly, and Annette Tagliaferro. The staff at Harper & Row were most helpful, especially Eleanor Jordan, who painstakingly read the manuscript and commented on it, and Joseph Montebello, whose interest as well as complete control over the production of the book was reassuring. I wish also to thank Everette Short, who photographed my painting for the jacket, Gary Gabriel Gisondi, who compiled the index, and Robert Lankford and Richard Stack who read the galleys.

A. S. M.

PROLOGUE

From the ancient gods of Egypt to the animated cartoons of Walt Disney, man's relationship with animals has been close, often intense, forming a bond even the advances of modern science cannot erase.

Zoo of the Gods explores this complex relationship through man's imagination as displayed in his mythology, folklore, legends, and arts. In a sense the book is a modern bestiary or book of beasts. It differs, however, from its medieval European predecessors in that it presents a world mythological view of its animal subjects, not just a European one.

World mythology is a vast subject. Reading its immense literature and viewing its myriad art forms reveals the amazing diversity of man's response to animals, whether in ancient Greece or in contemporary Pop culture. In exploring the nature of each of the more than one hundred animals in *Zoo of the Gods*—their mythology, folklore, symbolism, and cultural importance—this rich store of man's creative life has helped to delineate each animal's mythological profile. But the reader should be forewarned. Animals in mythology, whether real or fantastic, are hard to capture. They do not readily fit into a labeled cage.

Greek mythology and European folklore, for example, depict the wolf as a demonic being, perhaps best exemplified by the werewolf legend. Yet the same wolf in North American Indian mythology is creator of the world. In mythology, therefore, concepts of a beneficent being and a demonic one are not far apart. One animal often has the characteristics of both, sometimes even in the same culture. The lion, for instance, is a symbol both of Christ and of the devil in the New Testament. In later Christian folklore St. Anthony the Abbot is identified with a pig, the symbolic animal of the Egyptian beneficent god Osiris and his demonic brother Set.

Existing alongside, and sometimes coexistent with, the demonic-beneficent aspect of an animal is the character of the "trickster." The name designates an uninhibited, instinctual, and childlike character, whether it be an animal or an anthropomorphic god. Br'er Rabbit of African and American Negro folktales is one of the best examples of the type. Br'er Rabbit sets out to satisfy his physical wants regardless of the morality of his methods. In many ways the actions of the trickster animal relive man's dream life, where he satisfies his desires without regard to moral codes he supports in his waking hours.

Contemporary Pop culture also has an animal trickster in the character of Bugs Bunny, a Warner Brothers cartoon creation. Bugs plays all sorts of mischievous, sometimes diabolical pranks on men and other animals. In one well-known cartoon he lets a bulldog who has been chasing him fall from a clothesline by slowly releasing his paws. When the dog falls (not to his death as would happen in reality), Bugs comments to the audience: "I'm a mean bunny."

Audiences laugh at the antics of Bugs, for secretly they admire his amoral freedom and besting of a stronger, superior physical force. The reason for this may again lie in man's memories of early childhood, when his only desire was to satisfy his physical wants. A child, for example, does not understand the social restraints placed upon his immediate wants.

What the trickster, demon, and animal god or spirit have in common in all myths and tales are the human characteristics that the tellers of the tales have given them. The animals speak, love, hate, plot, and kill—in short, animals in mythology do everything man does. Of course, this could not be otherwise, since man is the creator of the tales, not the animals themselves. For the mirror placed up to the animal actually reflects only the holder's particular beliefs.

One of the most persistent mythological beliefs is that all forms of life possess some *anima* or "soul." The only distinction, therefore, between man and animal is in their bodily forms, not in their natures. By extension, if both men and animals share a similar *anima,* it is also conceivable that plants and such inanimate objects as stones all possess such a soul.

Animism, as the belief has come to be labeled, in part derives from man's dream life, where the boundaries of finite existence are broken down and in their place a new "liquid" order formed. A swamp reed is more than a plant to mythological man. It might be some transformed water nymph or the spirit of some erring soul now lodged in the plant. The eagle that swoops down upon its prey might be Zeus coming to abduct the beautiful boy Ganymede. As recently as the last century, some Pacific natives saw a group of Christian missionaries with pack oxen and they thought the oxen were the wives of the Christians.

When man believes in animism the whole world becomes pregnant with spirits, demons, and gods. These fantastic creations haunt all man's mythology since he calls them forth to make some sense out of his finite existence. It is only natural that many of the spirits, demons, and gods should be animals, since man has been in such close proximity to them, especially in societies that hunt for their physical survival. Easily then might a ravaging boar become a demonic god seeking vengeance on his offenders.

Zoo of the Gods is filled with these animal spirits, both good and bad, and with the tales that man has evolved around them. In interpreting the tales, myths, and legends, I have chosen a variety of "answers," ranging from ancient writers to Freud, Jung, and contemporary estimates from Pop culture. If some of my "prejudices" show in the evaluations of the various "answers" offered by different schools of thought, it merely indicates that some ideas are more congenial to me than others. Certainly the reader is not bound by my personal taste or particular beliefs. My only wish is that the reader find this journey through man's mythological imagination both entertaining and rewarding.

God had his dwelling in the great sea, and
was a fish therein.

Kabbalah

PART ONE

Animals of the Water

GOOSE, DUCK, PELICAN, AND STORK

There was a man who had three sons. He loved two of them, but the youngest, who was called Simpleton, he despised. One day the oldest son went into the forest to chop wood. His mother gave him a pancake and a flask of wine. While he was in the woods an old gray man came up to him and asked for some food and drink.

"I haven't any," said the youth to the little man. "Be off!"

The youth then went to chop a tree, but his hatchet injured him in the arm and he had to go home.

Shortly after, the second son went into the forest supplied with food and drink. The old gray man appeared again and asked for some wine and cake.

"What I give you I lose myself," said the second son. "Be off and leave me alone!"

After the old man left, the youth met with an accident. He cut his leg severely while chopping and had to return home.

The third son, Simpleton, now asked to go into the forest, but his father objected. Simpleton insisted, however, and the father finally let him go. The mother gave him a cake (made with water and baked in ashes) and a flask of sour beer. Just as happened to his brothers, the little gray man appeared and asked for some food and drink.

"I have only a flour-and-water cake and sour beer, but if that is good enough for you, let us sit down together and eat."

When they sat down the water cake turned into a rich pancake and the sour beer became wine.

"Since you have been so kind," said the little man, "I will bestow on you good luck. Over there is an old tree. Cut it down and at its roots you will find something."

The old man then vanished and Simpleton went to the tree, hewed away at it, and saw sitting among its roots a goose with golden feathers. Simpleton lifted the goose and took it with him to an inn, where he intended to stay the night. The landlord had three daughters who, when they saw the goose, were curious to know what kind of bird it was and ended by wanting one of its golden feathers.

The oldest daughter waited for an opportunity and then tried to pluck a feather, but she stuck to the goose. Her sister, who watched what happened, tried to free her but stuck fast also. The third girl, though warned, came up and stuck to the second sister. And so they stayed all night stuck to the goose.

Next morning Simpleton took the goose under his arm and went on his way, unmindful of the three girls hanging onto it. (We must remember he was a simpleton.) The three girls had always to run after him, left and right, wherever his legs carried him. In the midst of the fields they met the parish priest.

"Shame on you girls," he said, "running after a young fellow like that."

He reached out to touch them and stuck fast to the last girl. His sexton then stuck to the priest also. Two peasants who were called to help came up, and they stuck. An assortment of seven people were now following Simpleton and his goose, and still Simpleton did not notice them.

They came to a town ruled by a king who had an only daughter. Because his daughter had never laughed, the king made her promise to marry the man who could make her laugh. When she saw the seven people hanging onto the goose of Simpleton, she burst into laughter, and it seemed she would never stop. But the king did not like this intended son-in-law and set him various tasks before he could claim his bride. Each task Simpleton completed satisfactorily with the aid of the little gray man of the forest. In the end Simpleton married the princess, and when the king died, they possessed the whole kingdom.

This tale, *The Golden Goose,* a shortened version of the Grimms' telling, is common in Indo-European folklore. The goose was believed to bring good luck to the innocent and bad luck to the crafty. In a Hindu tale the wife of a Brahmin tore the golden feathers out of a goose and they became valueless. And there is the well-known fable from Aesop of the man who had a goose that laid golden eggs. Unable to be content with one egg a day, he killed the goose in the hope of finding treasure inside, but all he found was the goose's entrails.

Along with the ability of the goose to reward or punish existed the belief that it would spread alarm at the approach of an enemy.

When Rome was being invaded in the fourth century by the Gauls, the sacred geese in the Temple of Juno started to cackle when they spotted enemy scouts. The enemy soldiers grabbed the geese and killed them, but not before the populace had been warned. Later a golden goose was carried in procession to the Capitol in honor of the geese who had saved the city.

Throughout mythology the goose is connected with numerous deities. It is a symbol of the Greek Hera, wife of Zeus, in her role as goddess of fecundity. A goose is one of the three major gods of the Siberian Ostyaks, and the Finno-Ugric hero of the Flood travels in the form of a goose. Wild geese are sacred to Brahma in Hindu mythology, who is often shown riding a magnificent gander.

In popular folklore the custom of eating a goose in England on St. Michael's Day is sometimes said to stem back to the time of Elizabeth I, who on St. Michael's Day received news of the defeat of the Armada while she was eating a goose. But the story is apocryphal, since the custom can be traced back to fifteenth-century England when Edward IV ate the fat goose to augur the termination of the rainy and wintry season.

Often in mythology the duck is confused with the goose. The Hindu word *hansas* can mean swan, duck, or goose, and occasionally it is the duck, not the goose, that lays the golden egg in folktales. In one Russian tale, included in Afanassieff's massive collection, a serpent-witch turned a princess into a white duck when her husband the prince was away. The

white duck laid three eggs out of which were born three sons—two handsome and one who was clever and cunning. The witch killed the first two,
but the clever one escaped. The mother, anxious about the fate of her sons,
sought out her husband. The husband caught his wife by her wings and said
the magic formula: "White birch-tree, put thyself behind; beautiful maiden,
before." At this a tree rose behind him, and the beautiful princess appeared
in front of him. He then forced the witch to restore his children.

The pelican, like the duck, is a water bird, but unlike the duck and goose,
its mythological reputation is that of a pious, self-sacrificing creature. St.
Jerome says the pelican was known to restore life to its dead young by shed-
ding its own blood after the offspring had been killed by a serpent. He then
explains that the serpent was the devil, the offspring mankind trapped in
sin, and the pelican, Christ, who shed his blood to save mankind. Dante,
taking Jerome's interpretation, calls Christ *"nostro pelicano,"* or "Our
Pelican," in *The Divine Comedy.*

But the legend of the self-sacrificing pelican is not original with Christian
lore. The Egyptians believed that the vulture fed its young with its own
blood. The early Church Fathers, however, confused the pelican and vulture in their comments on certain Bible verses. Continually cited was verse
6 of Psalm 102, which reads in the King James Version:

> *I am like a pelican of the wilderness:*
> *I am like an owl of the desert.*

The New English Bible uses "owl" in the first line of the verse to maintain the parallelism; *The Jerusalem Bible* retains "pelican," but the *Revised
Standard Version* uses "vulture," perhaps pointing to the Egyptian origin,
though a footnote to the text says the meaning of the Hebrew word is un-
certain. (So much for there being one standard English translation.)

St. Augustine, using the Septuagint, a Greek translation of the Old Testament (he could not read Hebrew as Jerome could), comments that "male
pelicans are said to kill their offspring by blows of their beaks, and then
bewail their death for three days. The mother inflicts a severe wound upon
herself, pouring the flowing blood over the dead offspring, which instantly
brings them to life."

Behold here from the pelican's breast sprung
A stream of precious blood to feed her young.

Midmay Fane: *Otia Sacra*

Augustine's rendering of the pelican legend differs considerably from Jerome's telling, since Jerome maintains it was a male that restored the pelicans to life while Augustine has the male pelican kill his offspring and the mother restore them to life. If one used a one-to-one symbolic interpretation of Augustine's version, it is God the Father who kills and the Eternal Great Mother who restores life to the dead. This certainly, doesn't fit into the generally accepted Christian context. Augustine's version, therefore, was not the generally accepted one during the Middle Ages, when the legend was that pelicans were born dead and brought to life by the blood of their father. Shakespeare makes allusion to this when Laertes in *Hamlet* says (I.5):

> *To his good friends thus wide I'll ope my arms*
> *And, like the kind life-rend'ring pelican,*
> *Repast them with my blood.*

Shakespeare's use of the legend conforms with that of St. Thomas Aquinas, who in his great poem *Adoro Te* cries out, in Crashaw's translation:

> *O soft self-wounding pelican!*
> *Whose breast weeps balm for wounded man.*
> *Ah this way bend thy benign flood*
> *To a bleeding heart that gasps for blood.*

With Crashaw's version we enter the Baroque world where each emotion is intensified, bringing out all the sadomasochistic overtones of the original Latin poem. Although we with our rich lore of Freud and Krafft-Ebing view many myths and legends in a different light, it is still not uncommon to find the pelican symbol embroidered on the jackets of some young girls attending parochial schools. One popular Christian explanation of this practice is that the pelican has Eucharistic implications since "St. Gertrude . . . saw Christ in this form feeding mankind." In earlier art the pelican was always associated with the Crucifixion and often painted near the cross. The two uses of the pelican symbol, however, really do not contradict each other, since blood was considered life itself by primitive man, and

Christ's death on the cross as well as his blood in the Sacrament are life-giving to the Christian.

Symbolically, the stork shares with the pelican a reputation for intense devotion. Aristotle writes: "It is a common story of the stork that the old birds are fed by their grateful progeny." The Greek philosopher's statement was elaborated in the Middle Ages. The tale was that when the stork had grown old, his children would surround him, providing him with food, and aiding him when he flew by supporting him gently on each side with their wings.

While this medieval belief seems to have been forgotten today, the legend that the stork brings babies has not. Many Germans believe that if a stork flies over a house, it means a child is on the way. This belief, which is also held in other parts of Europe, may derive from the "stork-stones," or Adeborsteine, of Pomeranian folk belief, which holds that babies are either brought up out of the water or found in rocky caves. A child brought from a rocky place was called a stork child. The myth probably reflects the early belief that Mother Earth initially bears the child.

Germans also consider it good luck if a stork builds a nest on their homes, but Moroccans believe that it indicates the house will soon be empty. If a stork builds a nest on a tree, they also contend, the tree will wither. In European folklore it is believed that if a stork leaves its nest, it foretells a calamity. One episode from history bears this out. At the siege of Aquileia in 451 the Romans held out bravely, but Attila the Hun noticed that the storks from the city were leaving their nests with their young. He told his men: "See, the birds know the future. The city will surely perish." Attila attacked again and proved the storks right.

CROCODILE AND HIPPOPOTAMUS

One day a fat little hen was walking by a riverbank. A crocodile spotted her and thought she would make a tasty meal. The beast slid up to the hen.

"Brother, don't eat me!" the hen cried out.

The crocodile was puzzled by the hen's words, but his appetite got the better of him. He ate her anyway.

The next day another fat hen was walking by the riverbank, pecking for food. The crocodile, remembering how tasty yesterday's treat had been, went up to the hen and was about to eat her when she cried out: "Brother, don't eat me!"

This time the crocodile turned away and left the hen alone.

The crocodile decided to go to Nzambi, or Mother Earth, to ask what the hen meant when she called him "Brother." On his way to Mother Earth he met a giant lizard and told him what had happened.

"Don't you know," said the lizard, "all who lay eggs are brothers—ducks, hens, you and me?"

This African folktale portrays the crocodile in a much better light than most others, which usually show the animal as a demonic being. In another African folktale a crocodile arrived at a river and killed sheep, cattle, herders, and travelers. The people did not know how to rid the land of the destroyer until a fox suggested that they eat crocodile eggs to insure the enemy would not grow up.

In Egypt the crocodile was one of the most feared and dreaded of animals. When the canals dried up crocodiles would wander about the fields, killing and eating whatever came their way—animal or human. The Egyptians, quite naturally, identified the crocodile as a personification of the powers of evil and death, associating it with the demon-god Set. Yet the crocodile also served as a symbol of Sebek, another deity, who was in part responsible for the overthrow of Set in one Egyptian myth.

Such contradiction abounds in Egyptian mythology; thus we find crocodiles were worshiped in some parts of Egypt, while hunted and killed in others. At Thebes the animal was held to be sacred, and people would often put jewelry such as bracelets on tame crocodiles. At a crocodile's death it was embalmed. There was even a city in Egypt, Crocodilopolis, devoted to the cult of the beast. A sacred, tamed crocodile was kept in the lake by priests and fed cakes, meat, and wine. The priests would go up to the crocodile, some of them opening its mouth while others put in the cakes and other food. The meal would end with a mixture of milk and honey.

For the Arabs crocodiles served a useful purpose in the ordeals employed in the Middle Ages. An accused criminal was thrown into a lake of crocodiles. If the crocodile ate the man, he was guilty; if not, innocent. There were very few innocent people in those days. In West African belief crocodiles are the reincarnation of murder victims, and in Hindu mythology they are the reincarnation of murdered Brahmins. The Basutos in Africa believe that crocodiles not only destroy a man's body, but can take away his shadow or soul and drag it into the waters.

In European folklore, however, the crocodile is best known for the tears it sheds over its victims. A fourth-century bishop, Asterius of Amasia, took up the imagery when he wrote a sermon on fasting: "What does fasting mean to you except to imitate the crocodile of the Nile? These, they say, lament over the heads of the men they have eaten, and weep over the relics of the slaughter, not feeling penitent for what has happened but, as it seems to me, bewailing the lack of flesh on the head as unsuitable for eating."

The good bishop's grotesque imagination captures the general folkloric belief regarding the deceitfulness of the crocodile's tears. In Shakespeare, Othello says (IV.2):

> *O devil, devil!*
> *If that the earth could teem with woman's tears,*
> *Each drop she falls would prove a crocodile.*
> *Out of my sight!*

Along with the crocodile's tears, which do not exist, there was a belief that the beast had no tongue, which in fact it does. Herrick, the English poet, refers to this in his poem "To Mistress Ann Potter" when he writes:

> *True love is tongueless like a crocodile.*

The hippopotamus was also worshiped in Egypt, under a goddess whose name was Rert or Retu. According to some Egyptian myths the hippopotamus-goddess was the female counterpart of the evil god Set and the mother of the sun-god An-her. But on the whole the hippopotamus-goddess was a beneficent creature who guided the souls of the dead in the Underworld, which was a difficult journey beset by many hazards to the soul.

The dual nature of the hippopotamus in world mythology is completely suppressed in most modern mythmaking where the animal is often turned into a comic figure, such as the hippos cavorting to Ponchielli's "Dance of the Hours" in Disney's cartoon *Fantasia*. Here very fat hippos in cute skirts attempt to be graceful and beautiful—two attributes the animal lacks, not only in real life, but in mythology as well. Perhaps our modern view of the hippo may derive from our seeing the animal safely tucked into zoos, snorting and puffing, and where, deprived of its natural habitat, it looks at best somewhat ridiculous.

SWAN

Prince Siegfried, along with others of his court and peasants from the surrounding countryside, were celebrating his coming of age. His mother, however, was upset that her son had not yet chosen a wife. She informed him that the next day he must choose a wife from among those present at a special ball. The young prince, annoyed at his mother's insistence, was soon distracted by a flight of swans overhead. With a group of his companions Siegfried left the festivities and went to hunt the swans in the forest.

He soon found they had lured him into a thick wood by a lakeside where a gloomy, ruined castle stood. As he aimed his arrow at the swans, Siegfried saw them suddenly transformed into young women. The beautiful Odette, with a crown upon her head, stood out from the others. She told Siegfried that she and her companions were under a spell cast by the evil magician Rotbart. At night they were able to metamorphose into their natural form. The spell could be broken only by a youth who had never loved before and offered his love unselfishly to one of the maidens.

Odette so captivated the prince that he fell madly in love and swore to save her (a common happening in folktales). The evil magician, in the form of an owl, overheard the prince invite Odette to the ball at which he promised to choose her as his wife.

The next day the castle was filled with nobles; among them were six young ladies from whom Siegfried was to choose. The prince paid no attention to the young ladies, for he was wating for the arrival of Odette. Then an unexpected guest arrived, the evil magician in disguise, escorting his beautiful daughter Odile, an exact physical counterpart of Odette. Odile charmed the young prince. He announced that he loved her and that she would be his wife. The magician and Odile then vanished. Siegfried, upon realizing he had been tricked by Rotbart, ran to the lakeside in search of Odette.

Siegfried pleaded with her, telling her how he loved her and explaining that he had broken his vow because he had been tricked, and the maiden then forgave him. Rotbart, furious that his evil plans were thwarted, blew up a storm on the lake to drown the lovers and the swans. Siegfried and Odette selflessly jumped into the lake, thus destroying the magician and breaking the spell.

This summary of Tchaikovsky's magnificent *Swan Lake* ballet is based on the Soviet version which purports to be the "original" one. In other versions the lovers are destroyed in the end when their self-sacrifice comes too late to ward off the evil of the magician. (This is perhaps more nineteenth-century sentimentalism than folklore.) Tchaikovsky drew his ballet story from a German tale *Schwanensee,* which in turn reflected the numerous swan-maiden legends told in many Northern countries.

One old German tale tells of a nobleman who, hunting in the forest, came upon a lake and a beautiful swan-maiden. When he took the gold necklace she wore, she lost her power to fly away and became his wife. At one birth she bore seven sons, all of whom had gold chains around their necks. They inherited the power, which their mother had possessed, of transforming themselves into swans at their pleasure.

Swan-maiden legends are not exclusive with German folklore; they extend far back into Hindu mythology. The ancient Indians viewed the sky with its white cirrus clouds as a heavenly lake in which swanlike maidens, the Apsaras, lived. Their name comes from *ap,* water, and *saras,* from the root *sr,* signifying creatures that skim the water. The Apsaras would glide over the lotus pond of heaven, laying aside their feather dresses to become beautiful maidens. Like the Valkyries in Northern European mythology, these maidens took the souls of heroes from the battlefield. They also sometimes descended to earth and married mortals, but they often returned later to their natural home.

In Greek mythology swans were the birds sacred to the Muses, who were associated with the god Apollo. According to some nineteenth-century commentators on Greek mythology the Muses were originally nymphs similar to the Apsaras.

The best-known Greek myth relating to a swan concerns Leda. Zeus, in one of his many amorous moods, came to Leda in the form of a swan and raped her beside the river Eurotas. The girl then laid an egg, which when hatched produced Helen, Castor, and Polydeuces. In a variant version of the myth Zeus pretended to be a swan pursued by an eagle, and taking refuge in the bosom of Nemesis (goddess of retribution for evil deeds), seduced her. She then laid an egg, which the god Hermes threw between Leda's legs and hatched Helen. According to a Cyprian variation Nemesis, fleeing the pursuit of Zeus, took the form of a swan and dropped the egg from which Helen issued. Later Zeus put the swan and the eagle in the heavens to commemorate the event, almost as a modern lover collects photographs.

Swans were kept and fed as sacred birds along the Eurotas, where Leda was raped. They were also honored in Sparta as symbols of the goddess Aphrodite. In a late Greek tale Helen was united with Achilles on a spirit-isle in Northern Pontus, where they were served by swans.

Servant swans enter in the tale of Lohengrin, part of the medieval German poem *Parzival* by Wolfram von Eschenbach, though there are some earlier German versions of the legend. In the story the Duke of Limburg and Brabant died, leaving an only daughter, Else. On his death she was put in the care of Frederick von Telramund, a brave knight who had overcome a dragon in Sweden. After the duke's death Frederick claimed the hand of Else, saying she had been promised to him. She refused the offer and appealed to the emperor, Henry the Fowler, to have a knight defend her against Frederick.

Permission was granted, but Else looked in vain for a knight willing to come to her aid. Then far away in the sacred temple of the Holy Grail at Montsalvatsch a bell tolled, untouched by human hands. This was a sign that help was needed. Lohengrin, the son of Parzival, known in English as

Percival, was sent out though no one knew the nature of the mission. As he stood with his foot in the stirrup ready to mount his horse, a swan appeared on the river, drawing a boat along. Lohengrin then told the groom to take back his horse, since he would follow the swan. Trusting in God, he took no provisions on board, but after five days the swan caught a fish, which it shared with the knight. In the meantime the day appointed for the ordeal drew near and Else fell into despair. Then just when the lists were opened, Lohengrin appeared in the boat drawn by the silver swan. The knight came ashore, and the bird swam away.

As soon as Lohengrin heard the tale of Else, he volunteered to fight for her. He defeated Frederick and agreed to marry Else on condition that she never ask where he came from. Some time later, however, Else asked him. Lohengrin did not reply. On the next night she asked again but still received no answer. On the third night Else said: "Husband, do not be angry, but I must know where you came from."

Lohengrin at last told her that his father was Parzival. He then called their children to him and kissed them, saying: "Here is my horn and my sword. Keep them carefully. And here, dear wife, is the ring my mother gave me. Never part with it." At daybreak the silver swan appeared again on the river, drawing the boat. Lohengrin entered it and departed, never to return to his wife.

Wagner used the Lohengrin legend as the basis for his opera. He made various changes in the legend, however, to suit his artistic purposes. At the end of the opera Lohengrin sets forth to seek the Holy Grail and sings a long aria, telling the audience of his mission. Then in Wagner's rich, overelaborate stage directions, we read: "All eyes turn with anxious expectancy to him [Lohengrin]. The white dove of the Grail flies down slowly, and hovers above the skiff; Lohengrin perceives it, and with a grateful look rises quickly, and loosens the chain from the swan, who immediately sinks. In its place Lohengrin raises Gottfried, a fair boy in shining silver garment, from the river, and places him on the bank." Lohengrin then proclaims him the ruler of the land. Elsa (so spelled by Wagner), watching as the dove draws off her husband in the little boat, cries out: "My consort, My consort!" and "sinks lifeless to the ground."

The opera ranges from inspired to insipid, suffering from Wagner's tendency of being overlong as well as overbearing. Leo Slezak, the well-known Czech tenor who often sang the role of Lohengrin, once missed his cue to get on the mechanical swan as it moved across the stage. Slezak, famous for his quick wit, said: "What time does the next swan leave?"

TOAD, FROG, AND SALAMANDER

Giovanni, a cripple, had three daughters, Catherine, Clorinda, and Margaret. One day he set out on a journey to consult a great doctor to see if he could be cured of his illness. He asked his daughters what they wished him to bring them when he returned. Margaret, the youngest, asked for a simple flower. Her sisters asked for bracelets. Giovanni arrived at the physician's castle but found the building deserted. Dismayed that he had made such a long journey for nothing, he started on his homeward trip. As he left the castle grounds, Giovanni remembered that he had promised Margaret a flower, so he went back to the garden and plucked a daisy. Suddenly a toad appeared before him.

"Who told you to take my flowers?" said the toad. "Now you will die in three days unless you give me one of your daughters for a wife!"

The old man, quaking with fear, fled to his home and told his daughters what had happened. The two older girls said they would never marry a toad, even if it meant their father's death. But Margaret said she would go, since her father had plucked the daisy for her.

The toad arrived for the wedding, and as soon as he appeared, Giovanni was cured and could walk as straight as any man in the village. That night Margaret and the toad went to their wedding chamber. The toad jumped upon the bed and Margaret slipped under the covers. Suddenly the toad was transformed into a handsome young man.

"Don't tell anyone about this," he told his wife. "For if you do, I will remain a frog for the rest of my life. Here is a magic ring that will grant you anything you wish."

Time passed and the two other sisters sensed something was going on— for how could their sister live with a toad! They pestered Margaret until one day she revealed that at night her toad turned into a handsome man. As soon as she told the story, the toad became ill and was near death.

"Don't die, my sweet love," cried Margaret to the toad. She took the ring and wished for his recovery, but nothing happened. In anger she threw the ring into a nearby pond—and out stepped a handsome young man. The two lived happily ever after.

This Italian tale from Piedmont contains a common motif in European folklore: the transformation of a toad or frog into a beautiful youth. The Grimms have a similar tale in their collection called *The Frog Prince.*

Freudians have viewed the frog as symbolic of the penis. At first the penis is feared by a woman, they contend, but once she experiences sexual contact and pleasure, she realizes that the object of her fear is actually something desirable. Thus, the transformation of the ugly toad into the handsome prince. Their theory is interesting, except that in many of the variations of the folktale the frog is a woman, recalling its ancient role in mythology.

In Egypt, for example, frogs were considered a symbol of female fertility, as when frogs appeared at the annual overflowing of the Nile so necessary for the continuance of life in Egypt. Some Bible commentators believe this annual flooding accounts for the plague of frogs mentioned in Chapter 8 of Exodus. In the Biblical account, however, the frog plague is credited to Yahweh, not to one of Egypt's gods, and is one of the Ten Plagues sent upon the Egyptians. In South America Centeotl, a frog goddess with many udders, was the patron of childbirth. Women were sacrificed to her, again stressing the feminine symbolism of the frog.

Various charms used in folklore also support the female-watery aspect assigned to the frog. Toads and frogs are widely used in charms to draw rain from the heavens. The Aymara Indians of Peru and Bolivia often make little images of frogs as well as of other aquatic animals and place them on hilltops to induce rain. Other cultures, such as the Thompson River In-

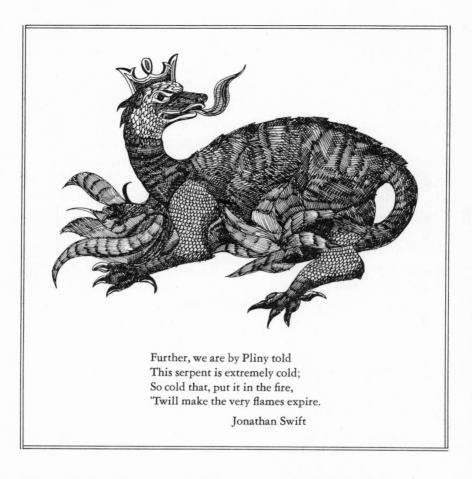

Further, we are by Pliny told
This serpent is extremely cold;
So cold that, put it in the fire,
'Twill make the very flames expire.

Jonathan Swift

dians of British Columbia, believe that if you kill a frog it will rain.

While the toad's association with water and female symbolism is widespread in mythology and folklore, in literature it has long been used as an example of extreme ugliness. King Richard III is called "a poisonous hunch-back'd toad" in Shakespeare's play (I.3).

Shakespeare's line recalls the belief that toads are venomous creatures whose blood, if drunk, would kill instantly. The antidote for toad poison (nearly all evils have a remedy in folklore) is the jewel found in a toad's head—the existence of the jewel being a common folk belief. Milton, for example, in *Paradise Lost* has Satan take the form of a toad to squat at the ear of the sleeping Eve and distill poison into her blood.

The salamander shares the toad's reputation for being a poisonous creature. There is, however, also a cure for salamander poison. If you happen to come into contact with the creature, or some enemy brews a drink made of the blood of the animal, all you have to find is a hairy stinging nettle, mix it with the broth of a tortoise and drink it.

The reputation of the salamander in most folklore and literature rests on some image other than its poison. According to Pliny the salamander "seeks the hottest fire to breed in, but quenches it with the extreme frigidity of its body."

Christian symbolists looked upon this belief and said the salamander represented the Christian fighting off the desires of hot, sinful flesh. They seem to have forgotten that according to the belief the salamander "seeks" the fires! Francis I of France was not bothered by the Christian interpretation of the animal. He chose a salamander, majestically sitting amidst flames, as a symbol of his absolute dictatorial powers. Under the animal's picture was the threatening motto: "I nourish and extinguish."

TORTOISE, TURTLE, AND CRAB

Indra, the sky-god of Hindu mythology, was under an unknown curse. His strength began to diminish, and all the universe was losing its energy and on the way to annihilation. The Asuras, the older half-brothers of the gods, seeing an opportunity, used all their strength to destroy the enfeebled deities. Out of desperation the other gods fled to the god Brahma for protection. He advised them to seek the aid of the god Vishnu. When they approached Vishnu, he said:

"I will restore your strength, but you must do as I command you. Cast into the Milky Sea some magic herbs, then take Mount Mandara for a churning-stick, the serpent Vasuki for a rope, and churn the ocean to obtain the Water of Life. To do this you will need the help of the Demons. Promise them some of the Water of Life—but I will make sure they have no share of it."

The gods listened to Vishnu and entered into an alliance with the demons to set about churning the ocean. They cast in the magic herbs, took Mount Mandara for the churning-stick, and Vasuki for the rope.

(In India a churning-stick is a stick with a long rope twisted round it. It is pulled alternately from each end. The rope holds the stick in a vertical position, while the turning caused by the pulling accomplishes the churning.) The gods grabbed the serpent's tail, while the demons pulled on its head. Vishnu took the form of Kurma, a tortoise, his second avatar, or incarnation, and became the pivot as the mountain twirled around. Vishnu was also present but unseen among the gods and demons, pulling the serpent back and forth—as well as being present on top of the mountain. He sustained the gods with his energy. When the venom from Vasuki burned the faces of the demons, Vishnu sent up clouds with rain that drifted toward the serpent and saved the gods from the scorching. After a long time the Water of Life appeared in a cup and the demons snatched it up immediately, ready to drink it. But Vishnu, assuming the form of a seductive woman, made the demons lust after him. While they were thus involved he gave the Water of Life to the gods, which restored their vigor.

This Churning of the Ocean, as the Hindu myth is called, presents the great Vishnu in his tortoise or turtle incarnation. There is some disagreement about which animal is designated in the text. The misunderstanding comes from the confusion of two Sanskrit words: *kaçapas,* or King of the Rods or Phallus, and *kaççhapas,* tortoise or turtle. In the transmission of the myth, *kaççhapas* was somehow substituted for *kaçapas.* The latter of course makes much better mythological sense. The white froth of the sea and the Water of Life that the gods and men need is the life-giving genital sperm, produced by the rubbing of a phallus at the base of the mountain.

The concept of water containing semen is illustrated in the well-known Greek myth of the birth of Aphrodite—who came forth from the foam that gathered about the severed genitals of Uranus, the Greek sky-god who was castrated by his son Cronus. The tortoise or turtle was one of the animals sacred to Aphrodite, as well as to the god Pan. Both deities were notorious for their sexual appetites in Greek mythology.

Ironically, Christianity has used the tortoise as a symbol of reticence and chastity. Perhaps these traits were attributed to a beast known for its slowness in the belief that it was less able to commit adultery or fornication.

This natural slowness of the tortoise is the basis of the well-known fable in Aesop. A hare was continually poking fun at a tortoise because of his slowness. The tortoise tried not to be annoyed by the jeers of the hare, but one day, in the presence of other animals, they agreed to a race. The hare was quite confident he would win. They chose a fox as judge, who gave a sharp bark and the race was on. Almost before the fox had closed his mouth the hare was out of sight—and the tortoise plodded along at his unhurried pace.

After a time the hare stopped to wait for the tortoise to come along. He waited for a long, long time until he began to get sleepy.

"I'll just take a quick nap here in this soft grass and then finish the race. There's plenty of time," he said as he stretched out.

Meanwhile the tortoise plodded on, passing the sleeping hare. He was approaching the finish line, in fact, when the hare awoke with a start. It was too late; and the tortoise was easily the winner.

Aesop's moral tag is "Slow and steady wins the race." Some Jungian symbolists have interpreted this explanation of the fable as an example of "natural evolution" as opposed to "spiritual evolution." The tortoise, they point out, is bound to earth, thus lacking higher, spiritual capabilities, unlike birds, who can fly to the heavens. What the Jungians miss is that the tortoise does win the race by sheer will, an enviable trait to be sure.

American Indian mythology, not bound by the moralistic Jungian or Aesopian explanation of the tortoise, believes the animal to be the creator of the earth. In one Arapaho folktale a tortoise or turtle swam to the bottom of the water, brought back pieces of clay, and formed the dry land. Chinese mythology, though not having a similar tale, has the belief that the tortoise is one of the four animal creators of the world.

No such high honors, however, are accorded to the crab, who often appears as a demonic being in world mythology. In Greek legend the crab causes havoc for Heracles when the hero combats the nine-headed monster Hydra of Lerna. The Japanese believe that the facelike form or imprint on the back of the crab is that of the Heike, defeated warriors who in the twelfth century engaged in a massive battle with another family, the Genji, and losing, did the only natural thing according to Japanese custom: they committed mass suicide by throwing themselves into the sea, where they were turned into crabs. Their faces were impressed on the backs of the shells. The Siamese go even further and believe that evil giant crabs drag down ships to their doom.

Why this disparaging view of the crab? Part of the answer may lie in the simple fact that it seems to walk forward and backward at the same time—certainly indicative to a moralist of an unstable personality.

In one fable by the early nineteenth-century Russian writer Ivan Krylov, a crab, along with a swan and a pike, set out to drag a wagon along the road.

> *It was not that their load was difficult to move;*
> *But upward strained the swan, toward skies above,*
> *The crab kept stepping back, the pike was for the pond.*
> *And which was right or wrong, I neither know nor care:*
> *I only know the wagon's still there.*

DOLPHIN, PORPOISE,
AND WHALE

After the god Apollo had slain the monster Python, he looked about for priests to organize a cult in his own honor. Spotting a Cretan ship making its way over the blue seas, he dove into the water, assuming the form of a large dolphin. Apollo boarded the ship and safely guided it to Crissa while the crew remained in abject fear, since they did not know what god or demon was in control of the ship. After they safely made port, Apollo took the form of a handsome youth and told the men to burn their ship and erect an altar to him there as Apollo Delphinius, or Dolphin-like. The men did as he requested. Then Apollo brought them to Delphi where he made them priests to tend his temple. The sign of the dolphin was carved upon the temple walls to commemorate the event.

This Greek myth, from the *Hymn to Apollo,* is one account of the god's designation as Delphinius. Another explanation says that Apollo merely replaced a local dolphin-god at Delphi, since Python, the monster slain by Apollo, had a monster-wife called Delphyne. This latter theory is perhaps nearer to what actually happened. Often one god's cult when replacing another god's in popularity would take on the attributes of the displaced god, in this case the name of the deity.

Another handsome Greek god, Dionysus, was also associated with the dolphin. As a youth Dionysus was abducted by a group of pirates who thought that he was the son of a rich king who would bring a large ransom.

The swiftest of all other living creatures...is the dolphin.

Pliny: *Natural History*

When they took the god aboard ship, Dionysus transformed himself into a lion. The crew in terror of the god dove into the sea and were turned into dolphins. Since Dionysus was an earth-god, however, the dolphin was rarely used as one of his symbols. But it was closely associated with such Greek divinities as Aphrodite, who was born of the sea; Poseidon, Lord of the Sea; and the Nereids, who were sea nymphs.

The dolphin's role as friend of man is found in numerous Greek myths and legends. One tells how Arion, a Greek poet of the sixth century B.C., on his way to Corinth from Sicily, was threatened with death by the ship's crew because they wanted his gold. He asked that he be allowed to play some music before he was cast overboard, and the men agreed. He played so sweetly that a band of dolphins swimming around the ship caught him when he hit the water and brought him safely to Corinth. In reward for their helpfulness the gods placed the dolphin in the heavens as one of the constellations.

A similar motif is found in the tale of the young Telemachus, son of Odysseus. The youth fell into a river and was saved from drowning by a helpful band of dolphins who carried him safely ashore. In gratitude Odysseus engraved a dolphin on his ring and emblazoned one on his shield.

In fact the dolphin has served many royal personages and ecclesiastical offices as a symbol. The Roman Emperor Titus used a dolphin twisted around an anchor to imply the mean between the dolphin's swiftness and the anchor's heaviness. In later heraldry the device of a dolphin was often used with the motto: *Festina lente,* or "Hasten slowly."

The belief in the swiftness of the dolphin as well as the numerous ancient legends of its helpfulness to man were not forgotten in the Middle Ages. The dolphin was believed to carry the souls of the Blessed to the Isle of the Dead in folklore. When shown with an anchor, it was used as a symbol of the Resurrection of Christ. (The anchor was often a symbol of the Cross in the Early Church, and as late as the seventeenth century the English poet-priest John Donne chose the anchor as his seal.)

Many early Christian paintings and carvings show a dolphin swallowing Jonah. This iconographic detail indicates the strong dependence of early Christian art on Greek and Roman models. Dolphins were often carved on pagan tombs. Sometimes the artist who executed the pagan work did the Christian work as well. Work was work, and religious differences mattered little to many artists, which may be shocking to some religious sensibilities.

The dolphin and the porpoise are closely akin and sailors often use the latter name for both. The dolphin was better known to the ancients, since porpoises seldom enter the Mediterranean. According to sailors, however, porpoises playing around a ship are a certain sign that a violent storm is on the way—whereas dolphins indicates good luck. Whales, however, were a certain sign of the devil to the medieval imagination.

Two legends circulated surrounding the beast. One told how the whale would lure fish to its mouth by its sweet breath and then eat them. Another legend (also found in the Jewish Talmud) told how sailors could mistake a whale for an island and board the monster. After they would make a fire the whale would begin to go under, taking all the crew with it.

Medieval imagination reveled in the interpretation of the two legends. Just as the whale drew fish to its mouth, one bestiary says, so does the devil attract by his supposed sweetness. (Often in medieval art the gate of hell was pictured as a monstrous sea creature's mouth. Freudians view the large womblike opening as a desire to return to the womb.) The moral appended to the second tale said that those who put their trust in the devil would be pulled down to hell just as the sailors in the legend.

Milton in *Paradise Lost* gives a variant of the legend of the whale island and identifies the whale with Leviathan, the primeval dragon in the Bible which Yahweh subdues. Psalm 74:14 gives this graphic description of the conquest:

> *Thou brakest the heads of leviathan in pieces,*
> *And gavest him to be meat to the people inhabiting the wilderness.*

Jewish folklore elaborates on the Biblical text, saying that at first God created a male and female Leviathan, but then realized that together they would destroy the earth. So God then killed the female but put her body in brine to preserve it for the Last Day, when God would serve up her flesh to the Holy. The male Leviathan would later battle the monster Behemoth, who resembled a hippopotamus. In the end Behemoth would be killed by the fins of Leviathan and the sea-monster would be killed by the tail of Behemoth. From Leviathan's skin the Lord would then make tents to shelter the pious, while the rest of him would be served up as a dainty dish. What was left of his skin would be used to make a tent to cover the holy city of Jerusalem.

In the Book of Jonah the prophet fled the Lord by boarding a ship. A storm arose; the sailors blamed Jonah and cast him into the sea. "Now the Lord had prepared a great fish to swallow up Jonah. And Jonah was in the belly of the fish three days and three nights" (1:17). The author of the Gospel according to St. Matthew, not satisfied with "great fish," writes that

Jonah "was three days and three nights in the whale's belly . . ." (12:40). This image was taken to mean that Christ would be three days and three nights in the tomb before he would arise. *The Jerome Biblical Commentary* says that if Jonah is to be interpreted symbolically, then "the prophet whose name means dove signifies Israel, the great fish signifies Babylon, and the three-day sojourn in the fish's belly signifies the Exile."

This interpretation certainly saves a lot of fruitless questioning as to whether a man can live inside a whale or not. Reality, so far as we know it, says no. But folklore and literature supply numerous examples of heroes living inside great fishes or whales. A Greek myth tells how Heracles was swallowed by a whale at a place called Jaffa and was inside the animal for three days. The Early Church, noting the similarity between the legends of Jonah and Heracles, said that the latter was an imitation of the Bible. We can see that both are common motifs in folktales.

In Walt Disney's animated film version of the Italian classic tale *Pinocchio* by Carlo Collodi, the puppet is swallowed by a whale. In the book, however, it is a large dogfish. Pinocchio and Gepetto, his maker, escape from the fish when it is asleep—because it suffers from asthma and palpitations of the heart and sleeps with its mouth open!

The most famous use of the whale in modern literature, however, is Herman Melville's novel *Moby Dick, or The White Whale*, published in 1851. The book was not a success initially and baffled most critics, who could not decipher its mixture of realism and symbolism.

Moby Dick centers on the pursuit of the great White Whale by the monomaniacal Captain Ahab, who had lost a leg in a previous encounter with the whale. At the end of the novel Ahab, in a boat with some of his men, shoots a harpoon, but it runs afoul, and the rope catches him around his neck, shooting him "out of the boat, ere the crew knew he was gone."

Some commentators on the novel view Ahab's struggle against the whale as an allegory of man's fight "against the malignant and imponderable forces of the universe, typified by the White Whale." Yet Melville's symbolism is much clearer in the novel. Many of the characters' names are derived from the Bible. The main character, Captain Ahab, is named after the evil king in the Old Testament who fights the god Yahweh by introducing the worship of Baal through the influence of his wife Jezebel. Ahab is killed in a battle in the Bible after numerous encounters with the Prophet Elijah, the champion of Yahweh. Melville's novel also has an Elijah who warns that destruction will come upon the crew if they sail with Ahab.

Is not then the whale a symbol of the Hebrew god Yahweh, who is terrifying and awe-inspiring, just as the whale is often described in the novel? Perhaps the final key to understanding the main symbolism of the work is in a letter Melville wrote that said most men "hate God" deep in their hearts. Captain Ahab had the courage to admit this and challenge God—even though the encounter brought about his destruction.

FISH

Manu, the Hindu Noah, was washing his hands one early morning when a small fish came up out of the water. "Keep me and I will save you," said the fish to Manu.

"What will you save me from?" asked Manu.

"There is going to be a great flood that will destroy all the creatures of the earth. If you follow my instructions, I will save you as well as the seeds of all living creatures from death."

"You are so small. How can you save me?"

"First, put me in a small jar filled with water. When I outgrow the jar, put me in a hole filled with water. When I outgrow the hole, put me into the sea. Then I shall be large enough to save you."

Manu did as the fish had told him. When at last it was put into the sea, it turned into a large-horned fish. Manu then recognized it as an incarnation, or avatar, of the god Vishnu. Matsya, for that was the name of the fish, then told Manu to build a boat and stow in it the seeds of every living creature. Manu did as the fish-god had instructed him. When the rains came, he tied a rope around Matsya's horn and the massive fish pulled the boat, keeping it afloat in the flood-tide waters. After the rains ceased the boat came to rest on the Northern Mountain, just as Noah's ark came to rest upon Mount Ararat in the Hebrew legend. Manu waited for the waters to recede and then made his way down the mountainside, which to this day is called "Manu's descent."

The phallic nature of the fish in this well-known version of the Hindu flood myth (there are numerous variations, one of which is narrated in the great Indian epic *The Mahabhárata*) presents the fish in one of its most prominent roles—that of restorer to life and savior of mankind. Thus we have the Buddhists calling their founder Dag-Po, or Great Fish, while the Hebrews designate the same name for the coming Messiah in the Talmud. Vishnu's fish avatar, however, best presents the phallic-savoir quality of the fish. The great-horned fish, which grows larger and larger as a penis does when it extends and expands, pulls the boat carrying the seeds of life through the primeval maternal waters. The fact that the myth stresses the great horn of the fish only intensifies its phallic nature, since aside from Vishnu being King of the Rods or Phallus, a horn is a symbol of the phallus in world mythology. Its nature is even stressed in the Hebrew Psalm 132:17, where the author writes, in *The Jerusalem Bible* translation, "Here, I will make a horn sprout for David. . . ." when referring to David's line of kings.

Vishnu's swim in the primeval waters further emphasizes the sexual symbolism of the fish. In Semitic-Babylonian mythology, for instance, the female monster Tiamet was both the primeval water and the mother. She, with her husband Apsu, brought forth the gods. She was eventually destroyed by one of the gods, Marduk, in a massive battle, after which he made the world out of her body.

The combination of the fish-savior afloat in the water is also stressed in Christianity. Tertullian, the second-century Christian theologian, writes: "We are little fish in Christ our Great Fish. For we are born in water and can only be saved if we remain in it." Here Tertullian is referring to baptismal water. It too, however, recalls the primeval waters from which life springs, since a Christian is born anew in baptism.

Christianity's use of the fish as the symbol of Christ is usually explained by the fact that each letter of the Greek word for fish, *Ichthus*, forms the first letters for "Jesus Christ God's Son Savior." But, as we have seen, the savior-fish precedes Christ and the adoption of the Greek acrostic. In Sumerian mythology the god Ea, or House of Water, the great giver of law and civilization, was a combination of fish and man somewhat like our concept of a mermaid, though rather more terrifying, since a human head lay under his fish head and human feet under his fins. Ea spent his days among men, instructing them in the arts of civilization, then returned to the sea every night.

The phallic qualities of the fish appear again in the tale of the Egyptian god Osiris, whose myth had a deep effect on Christian belief, as both Christ and Osiris are gods of resurrection. According to Egyptian mythology a fish swallowed the phallus of Osiris when his evil brother Set was hacking the body of the god to pieces. For this reason the fish was sacred in the city of Oxyrhynchites, as well as in other parts of Egypt. Yet because of this act the fish achieved a dual role in Egyptian religious thought. On the one hand, it was sacred because by eating the phallus of Osiris it had absorbed the god into itself, thus making itself holy. On the other, for the very act of depriving the god of his powerful attribute, the fish was an "abomination." The Egyptian hieroglyph for "abomination" was the sign of a fish, reflecting the belief. Priests of Osiris as a result would not eat the fish—because it was both sacred and an abomination (the two conditions often coexist in mythology).

At the same time, the followers of the Roman sex goddess Venus ate fish each Friday, the day sacred to the goddess, since her followers considered fish an aphrodisiac. Christians, however, ate fish on Friday for the exact opposite reason: they considered meat an aphrodisiac and fish the perfect sexual suppressant.

Popular urban folklore has added to the phallic symbolism of the fish. According to one popular lexicon, "fish" alludes to the female genitals since "the vagina has a piscine odor."

One doubts if Venus or any of her followers would find this designation acceptable, but Vishnu might smile slightly.

...The serpent was more subtle than any other
beast of the field which Yahweh God had made.

Genesis 3:1

PART TWO
Animals of the Earth

SERPENT

Yahweh God made all the beasts of the earth, air, and seas. Of all His creatures the serpent was one of the loveliest and strongest. He could stand up and walk like a man and was as tall as a camel. Of course, like all other beasts, he could speak as well.

When the serpent saw Yahweh God's new creation Eve, he lusted after her. Now the angels of God were opposed to Yahweh's creation of Adam and Eve. Satan, the head of the Fallen Angels, wanted to destroy the newly created pair, and the serpent agreed to help provided he could have Eve for a wife. From that day on the serpent often met Eve and talked with her. He even gave her a love potion in the hope that she would fall in love with him, but it had no effect on the woman. So the serpent decided to use his guile to bring about her downfall.

"Is it true," the serpent asked Eve, "that Yahweh God said you could eat of all the trees in the Garden except for the one in the center?"

"That's true," Eve replied. "We may eat any fruit in the Garden except what grows on that tree. We may not even touch the tree, lest we die."

Now Yahweh God had not said Adam and Eve should not touch the tree, but that they should not eat its fruit. Eve lied to the serpent and that was the beginning of her fall. The serpent then took Eve by the hand and led her to the forbidden tree.

"Touch it," he said.

And Eve touched the tree.

"See, you have not died," said the serpent with a smile.

Then he shook the tree and the fruit fell. He ate one, and picked up another fruit, and offered it to Eve. At first she held the fruit, looked at it intently, then began to eat the skin. Finally she ate the whole fruit. Suddenly Eve realized she was naked and hid from the glaring eyes of the lustful serpent. When she peered out from behind a bush, she saw the Angel of Death standing near.

"Yahweh will create another woman to take my place with Adam when I die," she thought. "I will die, but Adam will live forever."

Eve ran to Adam and told him what had happened. Fearful of losing Eve whom he loved dearly, he said: "If you must die, I will die with you," and he ate the fruit. Then Adam gave the fruit to all the animals to eat, which they did (all except the bird, Hoyl, who is still alive to this day).

When Yahweh God saw what Adam and Eve had done at the instigation of the serpent, he cursed the beast and cast Adam and Eve out of the Garden of Eden.

One day as Adam and Eve came out of the cave where they lived near the Garden, they saw the serpent who had tempted them. He was sorrowfully licking the dust and wriggling on his stomach, for he no longer had legs on which to stand. When the serpent saw the pair, his head swelled, he stood on his tail, and with eyes blood-red, made ready to strike and kill them. He ran after Eve, who fled while Adam looked for a weapon to kill the snake. Finally Adam grabbed the serpent by the tail.

"Because of you," the serpent said, "I am slippery and must go upon my belly, for Yahweh has cursed me."

Then in anger the serpent pounced upon Adam and Eve, pinning them under his massive weight. Yahwah God sent an angel to rescue them.

"My first punishment was not enough, I see," Yahweh said to the serpent. "Now, for what you have done, I shall remove your power of speech."

Instantly the serpent lost the power of speech and found he could only hiss. Then a strong wind arose and cast him to India.

This Hebrew legend, embellishing the Genesis account in the Bible with folk imagination, presents a motif common in much world mythology: the snake's responsibility for man's loss of innocence. In Persian legend the serpent also brings disease and death into the world. Ahriman, the evil spirit, by eating a certain kind of fruit (the Bible, by the way, does not specify what fruit was eaten; folklore names the apple, fig, and grape) transformed himself into a serpent and went gliding about the earth, tempting humans. His evil spirit entered the bodies of men, producing disease and death, while if his spirit entered the minds of men, it produced lust, greed, falsehood, slander, and revenge.

The Hebrew and Persian legends express the fear of snakes held by many cultures. In Egypt during predynastic times snakes would roam the countryside, wreaking havoc among the inhabitants. This generated the numerous inscriptions in the Pyramid Texts in which the worshiper prays to be saved from snakebite.

Egyptian mythology further reflected this fear of snakes in the monster-serpent Apet or Apophis, who was the enemy of the gods Horus, Ammon-Ra, and Osiris. Apet attempted to prevent the sun-god Ammon-Ra from rising every day, but the clever priests of Ammon-Ra devised a magic ceremony to guarantee the sun would rise. They made a snake out of wax, inscribed it with the name of Apet, and while reciting spells and incantations, cast it in the fire. The magic worked, for every day the sun did rise over the land of Egypt.

The same Egyptians, however, also looked upon the snake as a symbol of resurrection because it shed its skin. One Egyptian text, devised to help the dead achieve resurrection, puts into the mouth of the deceased:

> *I am the serpent Sata whose years are many.*
> *I die and I am born again each day. . . .*
> *I renew myself,*
> *And I grow young each day.*

The Greeks also used the serpent symbol for their god of healing, Asklepius, the son of Apollo who was killed by Zeus for bringing Hippolytus back to life. Asklepius was often shown with the caduceus, a wand of two entwined serpents surmounted by small wings or a winged helmet, both indicating quick movement. The symbol is used by Ukrainian-rite Roman Catholic bishops, as well as by the medical profession throughout the world today. The image of the snakes replaces the actual snake that was carried into the homes of the sick by Egyptian doctors to drive away illness. We have no record of the rate of cures effected by the Egyptian ceremony, but it might have been as high as some contemporary ones.

The beneficent aspects of the serpent are perhaps best developed in the Aztec god Quetzalcoatl, or Green-feathered serpent. He was the son of Iztacmixcoatl and his virgin wife Chimamatl, and had a twin brother, Tezcatlipoca. In an earlier incarnation as the sun-god (opposed to his brother Tezcatlipoca who represented night) he went down to the Underworld and brought back human bones, which, through sprinkling of his blood, were transformed into people.

According to one Aztec legend his evil brother Tezcatlipoca made him drunk with pulque so he left the land. Sailing eastward, he said he would return in the year Ce Acatl. Montezuma, king of the Aztecs, thought the god had indeed returned when in 1519, the year of Ce Acatl, Cortez and his army landed at Veracruz.

The Spanish missionaries adopted the Aztec myth and said that Quetzalcoatl was originally St. Thomas the Apostle who had come to convert the Indians to Christianity. Now the spirit of the saint had returned in the person of Cortez to complete the conversion of the Indians. Some of the Indians accepted the Spanish tale, some did not—all were either placed in slavery or killed.

The Spaniards were not the first, however, to adopt an alien myth to satisfy their own particular religious needs. The same stratagem was used by the followers of Yahweh in the Old Testament. According to the Book of Numbers (21:5–9) Moses erected a bronze serpent in the desert when the Hebrews were in danger of being wiped out by a snake plague. All who looked upon the bronze snake would recover from the poison snakebites. The image erected by Moses was similar to the one dedicated to the life-giving god Nin-gis-zida in ancient Sumerian ritual. The bronze serpent seems to have been in use for some time, for we are told that it was venerated during the reign of Hezekiah (717–686 B.C.) and destroyed by that king because "the children of Israel did burn incense to it: and . . . called it Nehushtan" (II Kings 18:4). The name of the serpent-god comes from *nehosheth,* or bronze, and *nahash,* or serpent.

Jesus uses the image of the bronze serpent when he says: "And as Moses lifted up the serpent in the wilderness, even so must the Son of man be lifted up: That whosoever believeth in him should not perish, but have eternal life" (John 3:14). Yet alongside Jesus' image of the serpent are the words in the Book of Revelation (12:9): ". . . that old serpent, called the Devil, and Satan. . . ." Some early heretical Christian groups worshiped a serpent nailed to a cross, while diabolical societies in the seventeenth and eighteenth centuries used the symbol in their worship. Some Christian sects today handle snakes in conformity with Mark's gospel (16:18), where Jesus says his followers "shall take up serpents."

Mythology supplies numerous cases of the serpent's connection with female divinities. The snake was closely identified with the Sumerian goddess Inanna, Queen of Pleasure, who was often shown holding snakes in her hands, symbolic of her control over the phallus. The Minoan Mother-goddess, who was the "master of men," was also pictured with snakes on her person.

The symbolic identification of the snake with these and many other goddesses has been fertile soil for the development of the snake as a phallic symbol. The symbolism seems to be maintained in a belief of the Plains Indians of North America, who hold that snakes will attack a victim from the rear during sleep, entering the victim's anus. Certainly, Freudians point out, this is a clear indication of the phallic nature of the animal. Even history seems to support this symbolic identification. The wife of Julius Caesar had intercourse with snakes, while one Roman legend tells how a snake visited a woman every night as her lover, returning in the morning to his den. Finally the snake was killed by the woman's relatives when they discovered the liaison.

Popular art has employed snake symbolism in the movies. In one film comedy of the 1940s, *The Lady Eve*, the heroine becomes hysterical when she finds the hero keeps snakes in his stateroom on board ship. The film's credits show a very cute snake (as only Hollywood can do it) surrounded by some very cute apples.

While there is much to support the phallic symbolism of the snake, Jungians speculate that the snake is a symbol of man's unconscious desire to destroy himself. This is diametrically opposed to the Freudian view, since the phallus is a life-giving force, not an instrument of death.

Initially, mythology might seem to support the Jungian view in the case of the Ouroboros, or the serpent devouring its own tail. Yet we find the cultures and religions that have used the Ouroboros view it as a symbol of eternity (a circle, without beginning or end) or as a sign of esoteric knowledge. The Gnostics, for instance, an early Christian sect, saw the Ouroboros as a beneficent sign, since through the snake man sinned and without the Fall from grace man would not have come into possession of the knowledge of good and evil.

Many other mythologies offer the head-to-tail snake as a symbol of water, the element that they believed surrounded the earth. Thus the Midgard serpent in Scandinavian mythology, offspring of the evil god Loki, at the end of time or Ragnarok was to fight with the god Thor and both were to be killed. Then a new world would arise.

With such a rich mythological history the snake emerges as perhaps the animal that most stirs man's deepest fears and hopes—death and immortality. Some of us then might agree with the first-century Jewish philosopher, Philo of Alexandria, who sought to combine the wisdom of the Greeks with that of the Hebrews when he wrote that the snake was "the most spiritual of animals."

APE AND MONKEY

Hanuman, the ape- or monkey-god of Hindu mythology, was the son of the wind-god Vayu and a nymph. He was so swift of foot and so reckless that one day he attempted to reach the sun, thinking it was a golden fruit. He leaped some three thousand miles but was unable to capture the sun. This attempt so upset Indra, the sky-god, that he sent a thunderbolt to destroy Hanuman. The bolt broke Hanuman's jaw, making his face appear apelike. This punishment enraged Vayu, his father, who almost destroyed heaven and earth but was dissuaded when Indra agreed to grant his son Hanuman invulnerability.

Although the sun adventure gained the apelike Hanuman this boon, he is best known in Indian mythology for his connection with the adventures of Rama and Sita in the epic poem *The Ramayana*. Rama's wife Sita had been abducted by Ravanna and imprisoned in his city in Lanka (or Ceylon). Hanuman and his apes sided with Rama in the great struggle to free Sita. After many adventures Hanuman reached the city of Lanka, which was girded by a golden wall and filled with buildings as huge as clouded mountains. Waiting till night, Hanuman entered the city as quietly as a cat, made his way to the palace where he found Sita, and informed her of his mission to free her. He suggested that she jump on his back and he would carry her across the sea to her husband. Although flattered by the rescue, Sita was afraid Hanuman's strength might fail and she would fall into the sea. She also told him she would not touch any person but her husband Rama and wished the glory of her rescue to go to him.

"But hurry," she told Hanuman, "and bring my husband to me."

Hanuman agreed to give Sita's message to Rama, but the ape's ego was bruised that he couldn't take her back himself. He decided he would destroy the groves and trees of Lanka and as many of its inhabitants as possible. So, as quickly as the wind rushes through the trees, Hanuman went on a rampage of destruction. Palace guards finally caught up with him, and as punishment Ravanna bound Hanuman's tail with cotton soaked in oil and set it all ablaze. But the heroic ape profited from his suffering for while he was dragged around the city as a captive, he noted every entry and exit so that he could later inform Rama.

When Sita learned that Hanuman was being led around the streets of the city, the woman was distraught that he had been captured in the attempt to rescue her. She prayed to the fire-god to cool the flames on Hanuman's tail. The ape's tail immediately felt cool, though it still blazed on. Then Hanuman broke his bonds and sprang into the sky, rushing above the city and setting it afire. Homes and treasures burst into flames. When he was finished with his destruction, Hanuman went to quench his tail in the sea. At the end of *The Ramayana* Hanuman is rewarded by Rama with the perpetual life and youth of a god.

The high esteem and importance of Hanuman in the epic poem reflects the prestige that monkeys and apes have in India's folklore. Even today there is a ceremonial marriage of apes conducted in some Indian villages. The festivities usually cost the village a considerable amount of money, which they spend gladly, though they may do without some food for the rest of the year.

But India is not alone in treating monkeys and apes as sacred. In ancient Egypt a dog-headed ape who assisted Thoth sat on the scales, weighing the heart of the deceased in the great Judgment Hall. When apes died, the Egyptians embalmed them as they did people and sacred cats.

China also paid respect to the monkey. A whole cycle of monkey legends grew around the adventures of a seventh-century Buddhist monk who traveled from China to India and back. The tales were written down in the sixteenth century. In one episode a monkey journeyed to the land of the dead and destroyed all the forecasts of when monkeys were to die—which is why monkeys live so long.

The ancient Hebrew rabbis had an entirely different outlook. According to the Talmud if one sees a monkey it is a sign of bad luck. One Jewish legend says three classes of men built the tower of Babel, one of which was turned into apes as punishment. The Moslems still believe that the ancient Jews who lived in Elath on the Red Sea were turned into monkeys as a punishment from Allah for having fished on the Sabbath.

European folklore reduces even further the animal's god-like status. All that is subhuman, shameless, and lustful is ascribed to the monkey in numerous works of the Middle Ages. One bestiary of the twelfth century says that while the monkey's whole physical being is "disgraceful, yet their bottoms really are excessively disgraceful and horrible."

Taking into consideration the medieval obsession with bodily functions, we can readily understand the medieval fixation with the anus. In treatises on witchcraft during the Middle Ages the anal kiss was equated with the kiss of the devil.

One nineteenth-century American clergyman spelled out the lesson of the ape for his young readers in doggerel contained in his book *Scripture Animals*, that goes in part:

> *Do Apes disgust, because the look and shape*
> *Bear such resemblance to the human form,*
> *While in the actions they are still the Ape,*
> *So wild and brutal, that they cannot charm?*
>
> *Ye bigger apes of human name and dress,*
> *Loose, foppish, vain, in manner much the same,*
> *Your near alliance to the Ape confess,*
> *Till worthier deeds shall prove a higher claim.*

The Reverend Jonathan Fisher's "poem" was echoed in numerous cartoons circulated when Darwin's *On the Origin of Species* was published in 1859. One drawing showed an ape being introduced as a relative. At about the same period the well-known plaster cast of the ape gazing at a human skull came into vogue.

The ape's closeness to man, however, is in more than mere physical makeup, according to Konrad Lorenz. In *King Solomon's Ring* he says monkeys suffer serious bodily harm from mental stress they undergo when confined. He cites that infant monkeys thrive when they are cared for by humans in a family situation, but pine away when they become grown and have to be removed to a zoo cage. Aside from dislike of loneliness, which is one of man's most distinctive characteristics as well, monkeys can literally become bored to death when alone. If the resemblance is not close enough yet—mother apes are known to display excessive love for their offspring. Folklore reflects this love in numerous tales. For instance, in one Aesop fable a monkey had two babies. The mother fondled one, while the other was ignored. One day the monkey who was loved and caressed was found smothered. Aesop's moral tag to the fable in one version is "Too much love kills the thing it loves."

Nevertheless the point of the fable was well taken by the seventeenth-century English author Richard Burton, in his wonderfully zany book *The Anatomy of Melancholy.* Among its more than one thousand pages can be found: "So parents often err, many fond mothers especially, dote so much upon their children, like Aesop's ape, till in the end they crush them to death." All this before Freud made so much of the mother's relation to her child, as if it were newly noticed.

With these common characteristics it is not strange to see modern myth-makers, such as novelists and Hollywood scriptwriters, using the ape and monkey. In the film *Planet of the Apes* astronauts land on a planet run by apes who hold humans captive and treat them as wild beasts. The script-writers must have read part four of Swift's *Gulliver's Travels*—and carried it even further by having the astronauts discover that they have actually landed on earth several centuries hence. The film version of *The Wizard of Oz* uses monkeylike attendants to the wicked witch of the West. One of the most popular movies of the 1930s was *King Kong,* which told of a gorilla in love with a woman.

Then there is the brilliant novel *His Monkey Wife,* by the English writer John Collier. It tells of the love of a chimpanzee, Emily, for a colonial schoolmaster. The final scene, where Mr. Fatigay and Emily make love, is . . . well, one must read the novel.

CAT

There was a woman in Connemara, the wife of a fisherman; as he always had good luck, she had plenty of fish at all times stored away in the house ready for market. But to her great annoyance she found that a great cat used to come in at night and devour all the best and finest fish. So she kept a big stick by her and determined to keep watch.

One day as she and a woman were spinning together, the house suddenly became quite dark, and the door was burst open as if by the blast of a tempest. In walked a huge black cat who went straight up to the fire, then turned round and growled at them.

"Why, surely this is the devil," said a young girl who was by, sorting fish.

"I'll teach you how to call me names," said the cat.

Jumping at her, he scratched her arm till she bled.

"There now," he said, "you will be more civil another time when a gentleman comes to see you."

And with that he walked over to the door and shut it close to prevent any of them from leaving, for the poor young girl, while crying loudly from fright and pain, had made a desperate rush to get away.

Just then a man was going by. Hearing the cries, he pushed open the door and tried to get in, but the cat stood on the threshold and would let no one pass. The man attacked him with his stick and gave him a sound blow. The cat, however, was more than a match in the fight. Flying at his adversary, the cat tore his face and hands so badly that the man at last took to his heels and ran away as fast as he could.

"Now it's time for my dinner," said the cat, going up to examine the fish that was laid out on the tables. "I hope the fish is good today. Now don't disturb me, nor make a fuss. I can help myself."

With that he jumped up and began to devour all the best fish, while he growled at the fisherman's wife.

"Away, out of this, you wicked beast!" she cried, giving the cat a blow that would have broken his back, only the cat was a devil. "Out of this! No fish shall you have today."

But the cat just grinned at her and went on tearing and spoiling and devouring the fish, evidently not a bit the worse for the blow. Both the women attacked again with sticks and struck hard blows enough to kill the beast, but the cat glared at them and spit fire. Then, making a leap, he tore their heads and arms till the blood came, and the frightened women rushed shrieking from the house.

Presently the mistress returned, carrying with her a bottle of holy water. Looking in, she saw the cat still devouring the fish, so she crept over quietly and threw holy water on him without a word. No sooner was this done than the place filled with a dense black smoke, through which nothing was seen but the two red eyes of the cat, burning like coals of fire.

When the smoke gradually cleared away, she saw the body of the creature burning slowly till it became shriveled and black like a cinder and finally disappeared. And from that time the fish remained untouched and safe from harm, for the power of the Evil One was broken, and the demon-cat was seen no more.

This Irish folktale, based on the version of Lady Wilde in her collection *Ancient Legends of Ireland,* presents the cat as a demonic being who can be exorcised only by holy water. One of the main features of exorcising the devil in the Roman Catholic rite is to throw holy water continually at the possessed person, causing the demon to flee.

In another Irish tale a priest simply says some prayers to accomplish the exorcism. The priest, who was dining with one of his parishioners, objected to the man's feeding his cat before feeding him.

"I am more important than the cat!" said the priest as he went over to the animal and proceeded to say a few prayers over the beast. Immediately afterward the cat went up the chimney in a burst of fire. When the saddened owner, who had loved the cat for years, demanded the priest restore his cat, the priest said more prayers and called the cat back from hell. Suddenly there appeared a fearsome cat covered with chains, nearly frightening the poor man to death. The priest dismissed the vision. The man then gave the priest some dinner.

One has the slight suspicion that this Irish tale was invented by some clerics to help maintain their control over their flock, since the priest was made into a "hero" who not only could recognize the devil when a layman could not, but could also destroy the demon through the proper prayers.

Lest we think, however, that only the Irish have demon-cats we find in Hungarian folklore witches who are transformed into cats at Christmas. According to Hungarian custom you must carve a stool starting on St. Lucy's Day (December 13). You work on the project until Christmas Eve. After Midnight Mass you go home, and strip down to your bare skin. Then you will be able to see the witches coming down the chimney in the form of cats. To make sure they are real witches and not just poor stray cats, you chop off their heads. If they are witches, human flesh will be underneath.

This Slavic custom of spending Christmas Eve is somewhat balanced by a charming Italian tradition in which a cat is supposed to have given birth to a litter while lying under the manger of Jesus on the first Christmas.

Yet even the Italians have demon-cats in their folklore. One tale tells of a woman who assumed cat-form at night and went about making children ill by touching them with her paws. The next day she would transform into human shape. Then, if paid sufficiently by the children's parents, she would work a cure.

An important characteristic of all cat transformation tales is that the cat turns into a woman, whether it be in Aesop, La Fontaine, or the great Hindu collection of tales, *The Panchantantra*.

The following is a typical fable from Aesop. One day a cat fell madly in love with a handsome young man. She begged the goddess Aphrodite to change her into a woman so she could pursue the young man. The goddess, pitying the cat, changed the animal into a beautiful girl. When the young man saw the girl he fell madly in love with her. The two lovers went off to a nice house and made passionate love. Looking down from Olympus, Aphrodite mused that now would be an interesting time to see if the cat's instincts had changed along with her shape. She let loose a mouse. At once the beautiful girl leaped out of bed and ran after the mouse, leaving her lover behind. The goddess, satisfied with her experiment, changed the girl back into a cat.

Freudians (whose mythology is as rich as any we will discuss) cite the cat as a symbol of female genital organs, just as the rat or mouse in their system is symbolic of the penis. They support their thesis with the fact that cats eat mice, symbolically seeing the penis disappearing into the vagina.

If this is too outrageous an interpretation, at least we do have to admit that from earliest times the cat has always been closely associated with woman. In Egypt the goddess Bast appeared with the head of a handsome cat. In one version of the goddess's name, Pasht, we may have the source of the common nickname Puss, though Webster's Third Edition does not see the etymological connection.

The connection of cat and rat is found also in the identification of the cat with Demeter, the grain goddess of the Greeks, who protected the wheat. Since rats are the natural enemies of farmers, a cat seems the logical choice as one of the goddess's symbols. Artemis, the moon-goddess of the Greeks, was also identified with the cat. She assumed cat form when the gods fled to Egypt to escape from Thyphon, the monster who had attempted to destroy all the gods.

Artemis' cat symbolism may derive from the ancients' belief that the waxing and waning of the moon reflected the widening and narrowing of the cat's eyes. (As with so many old beliefs, this one has been dispelled by modern science. We know that cats have an eye substance that, like thousands of mirrors, reflects each gleam of light and concentrates it. This makes cats "see in the dark"—though as with humans, they cannot see in total darkness.) The Greeks believed the moon created the cat, as the sun had created the lion. Clouds fleeing across the evening sky were mice being chased off by the flicking paws of the shining cat of the moon, according to a popular nineteenth-century interpretation of Greek mythology.

Because the cat is identified with several deities, it received a great deal of respect in most ancient civilizations. Perhaps its most honored position was in Egyptian society. Egyptians were forbidden, on pain of death, to harm a cat or to send it out of the country. When a cat died, the bereaved family would shave off their eyebrows as a mark of mourning. The cat was then mummified. A grand funeral procession took place with weeping and lamentation, until the cat was placed in a tomb with its favorite toys and saucers of food. This elaborate ceremony was not an exception but the rule. In the late nineteenth century some 300,000 cat mummies were uncovered at Beni Hassan and shipped to Liverpool, England—where the cargo was sold to farmers who used it as fertilizer.

During the fifteenth century there was a resurgence of the Teutonic cult of the Norse goddess Freya, whose chariot was drawn by black cats. The Church, fearing a revival of paganism, made an effort to suppress this "witchcraft." Many people were killed and along with them their cats. So many cats were rounded up and burned that the cat population in Europe dwindled considerably. In some countries the burning of cats as demons continued until the nineteenth century. The rite was usually performed each Shrove Tuesday.

Many cats had come to Europe with Roman soldiers returning from Egypt, even though Julius Caesar hated the animal intensely. The cat population increased during the Middle Ages when the Crusaders returned with them from their pillage of the Holy Land. Although the cat is famed as a long-domesticated animal, one writer, Konrad Lorenz, points out that the cat's chief charm "lies in the fact that, even today, he still walks by himself." This independent air of the cat probably figured in its having been selected as the symbol of the Roman goddess of Liberty. A large image of a cat was displayed in the goddess's temple, and a cat was shown snuggled comfortably at the feet of the deity.

Whatever independent or sacred air the cat carried to affect Roman and Egyptian mythology, it left an adverse effect on the Jews, perhaps because of the latter's contact with the Egyptians. There is no mention of the cat in the Torah. The word *chatu,* which does appear, is a Judeo-Aramaic word that probably means a polecat rather than a pet cat. There is one mention of the cat in The Epistle of Jeremy (v.22) in the Old Testament Apocrypha.

The old German sorceresses used on occasion to change themselves into cats.

Ernest Jones: *On the Nightmare*

It tells how cats, along with bats, swallows, and birds, sat on the bodies and heads of pagan statues of the gods. Since the gods did not act to remove them, the writer of the Epistle (it was not the Prophet Jeremiah) says the gods must therefore be false.

The Arabs, who inherited many Jewish as well as Christian beliefs and folktales, do, however, have a charming tale about Mohammed's cat Meuzza. One day the cat of the Prophet was asleep on his robe. When the Prophet got up to go away, he cut off his coat sleeve to allow the cat to continue his nap. Later Mohammed returned, and the cat showed his thanks by bowing to him. The Prophet then stroked the cat's back three times and conferred upon him and all his descendants the ability to fall safely on all four feet. Today if a cat enters a mosque, it is considered a sign of good fortune.

While the cat and Mohammed are friends in Islamic legend, the opposite is true in Buddhistic folklore. When the Buddha was sick a rat was sent for some medicine to cure him, but a cat captured the rat and ate him, causing the Buddha to die. The cat therefore was not present at the funeral ceremonies for the great man. Such an act by the cat did not endear the animal to Buddhists, who often cast the cat in a diabolical role in their fables. In Thailand and Burma, however, the soul of a person who at death has attained a degree of spiritual enlightenment enters the body of a cat. The soul stays with the cat until the animal dies and then goes on to heaven, the cat's body fulfilling the function of a purgatory. The connection of the cat with the soul (as the rat in Germanic lore) finds further expression in an ancient Thai burial custom. If one of the royal family died, a live cat was buried along with the body. Small holes were strategically placed in the burial site so the cat could eventually get out. When the cat escaped, the temple priests said the soul of the dead had passed into the cat.

Although many of these customs are not known in the West, Siamese cats are perhaps one of the most popular breeds. In a legend regarding the Siamese cat it is said that a god one day picked up a cat by the scruff of its neck, and ever since the shadow of the god's hand has appeared on the cat's descendants. The Japanese also have a tale regarding the black mark on a cat's back. They say it is the soul of someone's ancestor. The cat therefore should be treated with all respect and brought to the temple to be cared for by the priests.

It is thus not surprising that the cat has been a rich source for creative writers from the earliest fables of India to the poems of T. S. Eliot. Among the most interesting English poems is one by Christopher Smart, a poet of the eighteenth century who was quite mad. When he was confined in Bedlam, with only his cat Jeoffry, Smart wrote in part:

For I will consider my cat Jeoffry.
For he is the servant of the living God,
  duly and daily serving him. . . .
For having done duty and received blessing
  he begins to consider himself.
For this he performs in ten degrees.
For first he looks upon his fore-paws to see
  if they are clean.
For secondly he kicks up behind to clear
  away there.
For thirdly he works it upon stretch with the
  fore-paws extended.
For fourthly he sharpens his paws by wood.
For fifthly he washes himself.
For sixthly he rolls upon wash.
For seventhly he fleas himself, that he may
  no be interrupted upon the beat.
For eighthly he rubs himself against a post.
For ninthly he looks up for his instructions.
For tenthly he goes in quest of food.
For having consider'd God and himself
  he will consider his neighbour.
For if he meets another cat he will kiss
  her in kindness. . . .
For when his day's work is done his business
  more properly begins.
For he keeps the Lord's watch in the night
  against the adversary.
For he counteracts the powers of darkness
  by his electrical skin and glaring eyes.

For he counteracts the Devil, who is death,
  by brisking about the life. . . .
For he is of the tribe of Tiger.
For the Cherub Cat is a term of the Angel Tiger.
For he has the subtlety and hissing of a
  serpent, which in goodness he suppresses.
For he will not do destruction, if he is well-fed.
  neither will he spit without provocation.
For he purrs in thankfulness, when God tells
  him he's a good Cat. . . .

Smart's cat is not so well known as Lewis Carroll's Cheshire Cat of *Alice's Adventures in Wonderland.* Carroll's cat, with the grin that lingers when the cat disappears, has never been satisfactorily explained. One idea is that cheese was once made in Cheshire in the form of a cat's head.

The Chinese tell a tale about cats as the first rulers of the world. They could speak and ran the everyday affairs of the planet. Man then was a very lowly creature without the ability to speak. One day, however, the cats decided they preferred to sit in the sun and warm themselves instead of governing the earth. So they looked about and chose man to take their place. They had to give man the power of speech, which the cats in turn lost, and that is why they always seem to smile at us.

"Who knows," writes the French essayist Montaigne, "whether the cat is not amusing herself with me more than I with her?"

TIGER, LEOPARD, AND PANTHER

Once a tiger was caught in a trap laid by villagers in India. He tried in vain to get out through the bars, but all his efforts were useless. By chance a Brahmin passed by.

"Let me out of this cage, oh, holy one," cried the tiger.

"No, my friend," replied the Brahmin mildly. "You might probably eat me if I did."

"Not at all," swore the tiger. "On the contrary I will be very grateful to you and serve you."

Moved by this reply, the Brahmin decided to free the beast. Out popped the tiger, saying: "What a fool you are! What is to prevent me from eating you? I've been locked up so long and haven't had a thing to eat—and you look like a nice dinner!"

The Brahmin pleaded with the tiger for his life. The tiger eventually compromised. They would ask of six things they met whether the tiger had a right to eat the Brahmin.

The first thing they came upon was a tree, and they asked their question.

"Men are evil," the tree replied. "They break my branches. Yes, eat the Brahmin."

They moved on. Each tree, plant, or animal questioned sided with the tiger and said: "Eat the Brahmin." By then the tiger was very hungry and the Brahmin very afraid. Finally they came to the jackal, the sixth and last one. They told him the story and asked for his opinion.

"How confusing," said the jackal. "Would you mind telling me it all over again? I got so confused."

The tale was repeated to the jackal. As it was being retold, the jackal walked toward the cage and the others followed him.

"Oh, my poor brain," said the jackal, wringing his paws. "Let me see now! How did it all begin? You were in the cage and the tiger came walking by—"

"No, stupid!" cried the tiger, whose anger was fuel for his hunger. "What a fool you are. I was in the cage."

"How did you get in?"

"How? Why the usual way, of course."

"What is the usual way?" asked the jackal very innocently.

At this the tiger lost all his patience and jumped into the cage. "This way, you stupid jackal. Now do you understand?"

"Perfectly!" grinned the jackal as he dexterously swung the door shut.

This Hindu folktale, aside from exhibiting the cleverness of the jackal at its best, points up one of the most characteristic attributes of the tiger: its destructiveness toward man. So strong is this belief in the animal's demonic qualities that there is a special hell in Hindu mythology where tigers go after death. The concept is even further elaborated in Malayan mythology, in which an entire city constructed of human bones, skin, and hair is believed to be inhabited by tigers. The tiger has also been recognized in Western Europe from Roman times as a beast of destruction.

The Roman historian Suetonius, in his *Lives of the Twelve Caesars*, says criminals were thrown to tigers as punishment. Whether the statement is true is debatable, since much of Suetonius is closer to fiction than to fact.

With tigers actually available to the ancients for inspection, it is difficult to account for the numerous misconceptions about their natural habits. One widely held belief was that there were only female tigers. The father was the West Wind.

Just as unscientific was the belief that the only way to steal cubs and avoid being attacked by the mother tiger was to drop mirrors along the path of escape. The tigress would stop to gaze at the glass, admiring her looks, giving the thief time to be off with the cubs. If, however, he was not fast enough to escape, the tigress would make a feast of him. According to folklore she would prefer black men to white, though in an emergency a white man would do. (Racism also exists in folklore.)

The folklore surrounding the tiger is very rich, but the sheer terror of the animal has perhaps left its greatest mark on literature. William Blake's well-known poem "The Tyger" opens with

> *Tyger, Tyger, burning bright,*
> *In the forests of the night;*
> *What immortal hand or eye,*
> *Could frame thy fearful symmetry?*

and ends with

> *Tyger, Tyger, burning bright,*
> *In the forests of the night:*
> *What immortal hand or eye*
> *Dare frame thy fearful symmetry?*

T. S. Eliot, a later poet, calls Christ the tiger in "Geronation," again recalling the terror, strength, and awe that the beast conjures up in man.

The leopard, in reverse symbolism, has come to represent cruelty, sin, the devil, and antichrist. In one massive medieval mural of the Last Judgment the leopard is shown devouring the bodies of the damned. Often in Renaissance paintings the animal is shown accompanying the Magi who have come to the Christ child, a symbol of the eventual destruction of the devil by Christ.

The demonic aspect of the leopard might in part be traced to his earlier identification with two ancient deities, Pan and Dionysus, both disliked by the Christians because of their reputations for excessive sexuality. Pan in ancient works of art is often shown wearing a leopard skin, while Dionysus rides a chariot drawn by leopards. Titian has a marvelous painting in which he portrays the young god leaping from his leopard-drawn chariot.

The leopard, however, was not the only catlike animal in Dionysus' zoo. The panther was also associated with the god, as it was with other deities such as Ninurta and Osiris. Yet medieval symbolists identified the panther with Christ's Resurrection, because they believed the animal slept for three days and then emerged from its den with a roar that all the other animals could hear. From the panther's mouth came a sweet-smelling odor that enticed all the animals—except the dragon, who, upon hearing the sound, fled to its den, where it fell asleep from the panther's sweet breath!

The medieval symbolists worked out a very simple explanation of the legend. The animal's sweet breath was the Holy Spirit which came forth from Christ. This gift pleased the whole world except for the dragon, who was of course the devil and therefore fled to hell where he belonged.

STAG

There was a valley thickly set with pitch trees and sharp-pointed cypresses, sacred to the goddess Artemis, the huntress. In the recesses of this sacred place was a natural grotto, where a limpid fountain ran murmuring on the right, and its channels edged the grass. Here, when wearied with hunting, Artemis bathed her virgin limbs in the clear water. She would hand her javelin and unstrung bow to one of her nymphs. Another nymph removed her mantle; two others removed the sandals from her feet, while another gathered up her hair. Other nymphs poured out water from large urns upon the goddess. One day Actaeon, having left his hunting party, wandered through the unknown woods and came into the grotto.

As soon as he entered, the nymphs beat their breasts and the woods resounded with their shrieks as they fled to the goddess's protection. Artemis was taller and more beautiful than all of them as the rays of the sun danced upon her face. Not having her arrows at hand, Artemis took up some water, and sprinkling Actaeon's face, cried out: "Now try and tell them that you saw a goddess nude amidst her maidens!"

From Actaeon's head appeared the horns of a lively stag, his neck lengthened, and his ears grew points. On all fours, his hands became feet, his arms, long legs—and his body was covered with a spotted coat of hair.

Transformed into a stag, he took flight and ran to a stream, where he saw his reflection. He tried to speak, but his voice failed him. Only the groan of an animal came out of his mouth. Yet his understanding remained.

Suddenly Actaeon's hunting dogs, fifty in number, spotted him and gave chase. The young man's companions also joined the hunt and urged the dogs on. Poor Actaeon tried again to tell his companions who he was, but again his voice failed. The dogs gathered around him on all sides, sinking their jaws into his stag's body and tearing their master to pieces, finally appeasing the goddess's anger.

Ovid's retelling of the Greek myth in his *Metamorphoses* presents the virgin-goddess aspect of Artemis (whom the Romans identified with their goddess Diana) in one of her most unflattering roles. She is vengeful and cruel beyond the supposed infringement to her sacred person. Various explanations were offered by the ancient writers to account for the goddess's cruel action. Lucian, a second-century writer, in one of his satires has Juno, Jove's wife, say to Diana that the reason Actaeon was turned into a stag by the goddess was so the young man would not tell his companions that the goddess had a very ugly body.

We, however, cannot dismiss the goddess's anger as simply part of her vanity. In Greek mythology Artemis was not only a virgin-goddess, she was also an orgiastic nymph. These two roles often existed side by side in Greek mythology. In Artemis' role as orgiastic nymph the stag (symbol of male virility) was sacrificed to her.

Agamemnon killed one of the stags sacred to the goddess, causing his fleet to remain in harbor because there was no wind. Unable to sail for Troy, the Greeks asked their priest how to placate the goddess. Agamemnon was told to sacrifice his daughter Iphigenia. When the sacrifice was about to take place, Artemis substituted a stag for Iphigenia and took the maiden away to Tauris, where she became a priestess of the goddess.

The sacrifice of Iphigenia was the subject of one of Tiepolo's great paintings. The stag is shown on a cloud in the distance as the young girl is about to be killed. Tiepolo's sensuous forms and color capture all the richness of Baroque art, yet the strength of the Greek myth still remains.

Although the stag was a symbol of male virility under the control of a goddess, as in the case of Artemis, the animal also served separately to identify numerous male saints. Eustace, a second-century saint, was always pictured with the image of a stag with a cross between its antlers. Eustace was an officer under the Emperor Trajan. One day Eustace went out hunting near Tivoli and saw a vision of a white stag, who was bearing a luminous cross between its antlers. This mysterious sight brought about the young man's conversion to Christianity. When the emperor found out that one of his favorites was a Christian, he had Eustace and his sons (Eustace was married) roasted to death inside a large brass bull. Eustace's legend was applied to other saints, notably to Hubert, an eighth-century saint who became the patron of hunters.

One of the most interesting variations of the legend, however, is connected with St. Patrick. The great apostle of Ireland (who was either of French, Scottish, or perhaps even of English blood), on his way to Tara with a disciple, transformed himself into a stag and his companion into a fawn to avoid being detected by pagans waiting to destroy them. God was in a very merciful mood that day, since the pagans were not hungry or they would have slain the animals for food.

The great Gaelic poem *The Deer's Cry*, ascribed to the saint, is a survival of the pagan legend of a magic mantle used by the Druids to make a man or a woman invisible or transformed into an animal, as were Patrick and his companion. The magic mantle later found its way from the Druid legends to the shoulders of many Christian saints. Patrick's transformation might also reflect a remembrance of the Greek legend of Actaeon, only in the saint's case the transformation was at his will and for his protection. However, in Christian lore the stag symbolized the Resurrection of Christ.

According to European folklore, when a stag reached fifty years it would search for a snake, its natural enemy. Then it would place its nostrils against the snakehole and inhale sharply, sucking out the snake, which it would then eat. After the meal the stag would make a mad dash to the nearest pool and drink as much water as possible to renew its antlers for another fifty years. If, however, the animal did not get to the water within three hours after eating the snake, it would die.

What did this legend symbolize to the medieval thinker? The stag was seen as a symbol of Christ who rose from the dead after three days.

The snake, as always in Christian lore, was the devil. The fact that the whole legend does not tally with other aspects of Christ did not bother the medieval symbolist. For instance, if the animal did not get to water on time, it would die. Did that mean there was a greater power than Christ?

To avoid this question the stag was also used to symbolize the Christian, who if he did not drink of the waters of Baptism would die. This interpretation was reinforced in medieval imagination by the use of stags in early Christian art around a fountain. Verification of the symbolism was found in the opening verse of Psalm 42:

> *As the hart panteth after the water brooks,*
> *So panteth my soul after thee, O God.*

If there are still many questions unanswered in the symbolic interpretation, the fault is ours. One-to-one relationships have so conditioned us that when we encounter an imagination without our limitations, we tend to scoff at it. But should we?

HORSE

Phaeton was the son of Apollo and Clymene. The boy was taunted by a playmate, Ephaus, who did not believe Phaeton was the son of a god. So the boy went to the palace of his father. Arrayed in purple garments, Apollo was seated on a throne sparkling with brilliant emeralds. On his right hand and on his left the Days, the Months, the Years, the Ages, the Hours, the Seasons were arranged.

"Why have you come here?" the god asked.

"No one believes that I am your son," the boy replied.

The god removed the shining rays from around his head, went up to the boy, and embraced him.

"Certainly you are my dear son," the god said. "Ask any gift of your father, and by the sacred river I will grant it to you."

Without a moment's hesitation the boy asked for the loan of his father's chariot and its four winged horses for one day. The father tried to dissuade the boy from so perilous a journey, as even Zeus himself had not mastered the horses. But Phaeton was all the more excited and Apollo could not go back on his promise. The boy was led to the chariot and horses. Apollo touched the face of his son with a holy drug so he could endure the burning flames. He then gave him the rays to place upon his hair.

"At least listen to your father in this—be sparing with the whip and use the bridle with nerve," the god said, and then he instructed Phaeton to follow the usual paths across the heavens.

Phaeton sprang into the chariot, grasped the reins, and thanked his father. The horses filled the air with their snortings and fiery breath as they stamped the ground. Before Phaeton lay the boundless plain of the entire universe. The horses began their journey, but as soon as they perceived that they were being driven by a weak hand, they rushed off the beaten track. Phaeton became alarmed as he tried to control the stampeding horses.

He looked down upon the earth, far beneath his frail body, and his knees began to give way in sheer fright. He imagined he saw strange objects scattered everywhere throughout the heavens. He saw a spot where the Scorpion bends its arms into two curves, and with its tail and claws bending on either side, extends its limbs through the space of two signs of the zodiac. As soon as Phaeton beheld the Scorpion wet with the sweat of black venom and the barbed point of its tail, the boy let go of the reins. Now completely out of control, the horses carried the fiery chariot off its course and soon the entire heavens began to flame. The earth also caught fire, and it seemed as if the universe would blaze to an end.

The earth cried out to Zeus for help, and the god sent a thunderbolt to strike Phaeton. Flames consumed his yellow hair and young body; the chariot broke into a thousand pieces. Phaeton's charred body was buried by the Hesperian Naiads, who inscribed this verse over it:

> *Here he, who drove the sun's bright chariot, lies;*
> *His father's fiery steeds he could not guide,*
> *But in the glorious enterprise he died.*

Phaeton's disastrous ride, described by Ovid in his *Metamorphoses,* is perhaps one of the most vivid stories in that poet's work. It has been variously interpreted. St. John Chrysostom suggests it was a pagan version of Elijah's fiery ascent to heaven in a chariot as described in the Old Testament (II Kings 2:11). Plutarch writes that Phaeton was a king of the Molossians who drowned himself in the Po after having warned his people that excessive heat would destroy his kingdom.

The descriptive power of Ovid's verse—with the horses racing across the sky—inspired the French composer Saint-Saëns' symphonic poem *Phaeton's Ride*, a beautiful piece of nineteenth-century Romantic music. The motif of a ride through the heavens also gave impetus later to Sibelius' tone poem *Nightride and Sunrise.*

Apollo's ride across the heavens is repeated in numerous other mythologies. The Rhodians, who worshiped the sun as their chief divinity, dedicated a chariot and four horses to him, which they then flung into the sea for the god's use. They repeated this custom each year, perhaps in the belief that only young horses and a new chariot were worthy of the god. The Spartans also sacrificed horses to the sun on Mount Taygetus, where they could watch the sun set. Even the kings of Judah in the Old Testament (II Kings 23:11) dedicated statues of chariots and horses to the sun, against the direction of the Hebrew Prophets. The statues were later destroyed as idolatrous. In Hindu mythology Dadhikra, a winged horse, represented the majesty of the setting sun.

One of the most interesting tales relating to the horse is found in Nordic mythology. The gods had entered into an agreement with a giant to build walls to surround their home, Asgard. The giant agreed to do the work in one winter if he could have as payment the goddess Freya as his wife, as well as the sun and the moon. The gods agreed, thinking the giant would never finish the task on time and they would have the work for nothing. The giant, however, brought a horse called Svadilfari, who was so intelligent and swift that the wall was soon but three days' away from completion. But Loki, a trickster god, came up with a plan. He took the form of a mare and neighed at the stallion, thus luring him away from the work. The wall was left incomplete and Thor, the great thunder god, feeling he owed nothing to the giant, killed the giant with his hammer.

The union of the stallion and Loki produced the eight-legged horse Sleipnir who carried the god Odin in his journey across the sky to the land of the dead. The fear induced by Odin's death-ride was so great that farmers in the countryside would leave a sheaf of grain from their crops as fodder for the horse.

Odin was assisted in his gruesome task by the Valkyries, or Choosers of the Slain, female spirits who waited to take the slain warriors to Valhalla, where they awaited the last great battle between the gods and the giants.

These fierce warrior-maidens derive from an early Nordic belief that female spirits under the control of a war-god stirred up strife, took part in battle, and ate the bodies of slain warriors.

Wagner's second opera for his *Ring of the Nibelung* cycle, *Die Walküre*, tells the tale of one of these maidens who went against her father, Wotan (the Germanic name for Odin), and as a result lost her godlike powers. The symphonic-picture, "The Ride of the Valkyries," often excerpted from the opera, presents a graphic picture of the warrior-maidens' ride across the sky. An old Norse poem, which in part influenced Wagner's turgid verse, also captures the terror of the ride— and ends with

> *Start we swiftly with steeds unsaddled—*
> *hence to battle with brandished swords!*

In Iceland Odin's cult was matched by that of the goddess Freya, who had a stallion, which was not allowed to be ridden by anyone on pain of death. Half of those who fell in battle belonged to Freya and the other half to Odin, though the goddess assigned the seats to the slain warriors in Valhalla.

When Christianity infiltrated the Northland, Freya was turned into a witch and consigned to the mountains, where her followers would dance on Valpurgisnach. During the Middle Ages Scandinavia was in fact only nominally Christian, and the pagan custom of forcing horses into combat in the belief they would insure good crops was still practiced by Christians.

Christianity had used the horse as a symbol of death in the Book of Revelation where four horsemen are agents of destruction—two being symbols of war and two of famine and pestilence. The first rider appears on a white horse, the second on a red one, the third on a black, and the fourth "a pale horse; and his name that sat on him was death" (6:8).

This eerie picture influenced the Spanish novelist Vicente Blasco-Ibáñez in his novel *The Four Horsemen of the Apocalypse,* published in 1916. This family chronicle ends with the destruction of the German branch of the family in World War I.

Besides its connection with death in so many mythologies the horse is also associated with sexual virility. In medieval France, for instance, it was believed that mistresses of priests were turned into black mares at their death. Jung, taking note of the numerous sexual references to the horse in mythology as well as in his patients' nightmares, says sexual assault is often represented by a horse "that throws the dreamer to the ground and kicks her in the stomach with his hind legs."

Robinson Jeffers, in his narrative poem *Roan Stallion,* set in the mountains near Monterey, California, tells of the passionate love of a woman for a magnificent horse. When the horse kills the brutal husband of the woman, she shoots the beast "out of some obscure human fidelity," though she feels she "has killed God."

These feelings of the godlike nature of the horse are reflected in numerous mythologies. In Hindu myth the tenth incarnation of Vishnu, the white-steed Kalki, is to come to judge the world at the end of Yuga, the fourth and last cycle of the 1,800,000 years in the Hindu concept of the world. He will destroy the wicked, reward the good, and enable Vishnu to create a new world. This hope is also expressed in a contemporary Yiddish poem by Abraham Reisen titled "O Quickly, Messiah," which ends with a plea for the Messiah to come on his "silvery steed."

Pop culture has one of its heroes, The Lone Ranger, also ride a silvery steed, but he is a far cry from the concept of the Jewish Messiah, since he is nothing more than a self-appointed law enforcer who hides behind a mask —a concept that is no longer acceptable either religiously or morally.

BEAR

The King of Rocc'Aspra had a very lovely wife. But as death comes to everyone, beautiful or ugly, so it came to the queen. As she lay on her death-bed, she called her husband to her side.

"I know that you have loved me very much," she said. "Now promise me that when I die you will not marry another woman unless she is as lovely as I am. If you do less, I will curse you."

Hardly had the queen finished speaking when her spirit fled, and there was just time enough for the king to agree to her demand. After some time the king wanted to remarry, though he remembered his wife's threat to curse him if he chose a wife who was not so lovely as she. He gathered together his courtiers and made a proclamation throughout the world, asking that all the most beautiful women come to his palace so that one might be chosen queen.

Women from all walks of life came, but none was so beautiful as the dead queen. Then the king thought to himself, "Why am I wasting time on these ugly witches—when I have a daughter Presioza who is every bit as lovely as her mother!" So he decided to marry his daughter. Although the king had no qualms about incest, his daughter was horrified at the prospect, but to no avail. Wedding plans were set and Presioza waited unhappily in her room for the evil day. Then an old woman who served her told the girl not to worry.

"Every evil has a remedy," said the old woman, "except death."

She then told Presioza how to escape her father's clutches. Presioza was to place in her mouth a piece of wood when her father-husband came to sleep with her. The piece of wood would instantly work its magic, and Presioza would turn into a she-bear. In that state she could flee and live with the animals in the forest. To return to human shape she had only to remove the wood from her mouth to be instantly retransformed. Certainly the procedure was simple enough.

After a great deal of festivity the time came for the king to retire to the marriage chamber and enjoy his new wife. When he approached Presioza, she put the wood in her mouth, changed into a she-bear, and so frightened the king that he hid in the corner of the bed, afraid to move or peep from under the covers.

Presioza fled to the forest where she lived among the other animals. One day a king's son spotted her, and upon seeing how lovely a she-bear she was, he decided to bring her back to his palace to live. As time passed he fell in love with the sweet bear. One day he observed from a distance the she-bear transform herself into a beautiful girl. But before he could reach her Presioza became afraid and put the wood back in her mouth. The prince, sad because he could not requite his love, took to his bed and cried over and over, "Oh, my bear, my bear!"

His mother, thinking that the she-bear had in some way injured her son, ordered the servants to kill the animal. But they loved the bear so much they let her loose in the forest, telling the queen that she had been killed. When the prince heard what had happened, he wanted to kill all the servants, until they revealed the bear to be alive in the forest. At this news the prince left his sickbed. He found and brought Presioza back to the palace to live in his quarters. The she-bear now waited upon his every wish. She cleaned, served food, washed—in short, she became the obedient, subservient wife beloved in the Latin culture which is the source of this tale.

She was all things to the prince, except there were no sexual relations between them. Driven almost mad with passion, the prince one day grabbed the bear and kissed her on the lips. The wood piece fell out of her mouth and immediately she was a young girl again. She told her tale and the two were later married. His mother must have approved, for we hear they all lived happily ever after.

The transformation of Presioza in this Neapolitan tale, as well as a man falling in love with an animal or vice versa, is found often in mythology and folklore. In many North American Indian tales a man has a bear for his wife, although often the story does not end happily as in the Italian tale. In one typical tale a young man met a woman who was a black bear. He brought her home to live with him but later was unfaithful to her, falling in love with a former sweetheart. His bear-wife, heartbroken at his cruelty, left to live in the forest again.

American Indians looked upon the bear with awe and respect. When an Indian killed a bear, he would beg its pardon and often smoke a peace pipe so the bear's spirit would not be angry. This respectful approach reflects the American Indians' belief that the bear possessed great curative powers. Indian shamans in some tribes would imitate the bear in order to possess its rich curative powers. It was believed by many American Indians that shamans could transform themselves into bears and when they died went to the heaven of bears.

One of the most important aspects of bear worship among the American Indians was the bear dance. The Plains Cree Indians, for instance, would wear bearskins in the dance to restore health or ward off evil. We find also that the cult of the bear was part of the ritual of the followers of the Greek goddess Artemis. At her shrine in Arcadia girls between five and ten years, called "brown bears," would dance in honor of the goddess.

In one myth Artemis, in her role as defender of chastity, discovered that one of her followers, Callisto, was no longer a virgin, since the girl's obvious pregnancy gave her away. For violating the taboo against intercourse with men the goddess turned Callisto into a she-bear. Later Callisto was killed either by Artemis, who mistook her for a real bear, or by the son she bore, who years later killed her in the hunt.

In a variant of the legend, Zeus seduced Callisto while disguised as Artemis. After the two had enjoyed some Lesbian foreplay Zeus suddenly turned into his male shape and raped the girl. Zeus impregnated Callisto. (The head male deity could do no less.) Hera, ever-jealous wife of Zeus, found out and punished the girl by changing her into a bear.

In both tales Callisto had a son named Arcas. Since he was reared without his mother, who was in the forest in the shape of a bear, he was brought up by his grandfather Lycaon (whose werewolf transformation we will read about later on), who killed the boy to test Zeus by serving up the boy's

And by degrees she fashions out the paws,
The head, and neck, and finally doth bring
To a perfect beast that first deformed thing.

Du Bartas: *Divine Weeks and Works*

flesh. Zeus, however, brought the boy back to life. Later Arcas, while hunting, saw the she-bear, and not knowing it was his mother, pursued her to the sacred precinct of Zeus on Mount Lycaeus. For violating the taboo of trespassing on the sacred mountain both were punished. Zeus placed them in the heavens as a constellation of the Great Bear and Little Bear. This move upset Hera, who then complained to Oceanus and Tethys, the sea-gods, that she would not tolerate such glorification for a mistress of her husband. The two gods agreed with Hera, so the constellation of Callisto and her son never enters their realm as the other constellations do when they set. The Great Bear revolves constantly around the North Star.

Although medieval Europeans were familiar with the bear signs in the heavens and spent a good deal of speculation on interpreting them, their main concern about the bear symbolically was not its place in the heavens, but the manner of its birth. The most persistent folk belief was that cubs were born shapeless white lumps of flesh, a little larger than a mouse, without eyes or hair. The mother bear would lick this mass into shape, eventually forming a bear cub.

The legend was seen as a symbol of the Church converting the unbeliever to the "true faith." What was passed over in this symbolic reading were the references to the bear as a symbol of cruelty in the Old Testament Book of Daniel (7:5).

One can see a remembrance of the medieval concept of the bear in the character of Smokey the Bear, who tries to convert the absent-minded or unthinking camper to put out all fires before he wends his way home with his wife, kids, dog, and a case of poison ivy.

LION

A lion went hunting with a fox, a jackal, and a wolf. They finally found a stag, pounced upon it, and killed the animal. As the stag lay dead in the midst of the four, they each thought how it was to be divided.

"Cut the stag into four parts," the lion roared.

The others, obedient to the lion's voice, skinned the animal and cut it into four sections. Then the lion stood in front of the carcass.

"The first quarter is mine in my role as King of the Beasts," the lion said. "The second quarter is mine as arbiter in the case," he continued, "and the third share comes to me for my part in the chase. As for the last quarter, which one of you will dare lay a hand on it?" Hence the expression "the lion's share."

The others stared at the lion in amazement and fear. The fox mumbled under his breath as he walked away, his tail between his legs, quickly followed by the wolf and the jackal.

This tale, found in Aesop and in Oriental collections as well, presents the lion as King of the Beasts, one of the most prominent aspects of its personality in world mythology. This is due to the belief that the animal is a symbol of the sun. For instance, Mithras, the Persian god of light, whose name means "friend," had the lion as one of his animals. Mithras was often shown killing a bull, the symbol of lower, demonic forces in the world.

In Egypt it was believed the lion presided over the annual flooding of the Nile because it coincided with the entry of the sun into the zodiac sign of Leo during the dog days. Someone born under that sign is considered "very faithful" but "itching to rule and sway" over other men, according to a seventeenth-century English horoscope.

The lion's identification with the sun coexisted with another important role, that of destroyer. The Egyptian war-goddess Sekhmet, "the powerful one," bore a lion's head, while the fourth incarnation of Vishnu in Hindu mythology was as the man-lion, Narasinha, who destroyed a man who did not believe in his power. In the New Testament the author of First Peter (5:8) tells his readers to be on guard against the devil, who "as a roaring lion, walketh about, seeking whom he may devour."

Yet alongside this designation of the lion as the devil we have the author of the Book of Revelation (5:5) writing of Jesus Christ: "Behold, the Lion of the tribe of Juda, the Root of David, hath prevailed to open the book, and to loose the seven seals thereof." The author of this passage is recalling the numerous references in the Old Testament where the lion is used as a symbol of kingly power and ferocity. To explain this contradiction in Scripture, however, St. Gregory the Great says one element can have more than one symbolic meaning in the Bible.

The demonic role of the lion, however, was still felt in the Middle Ages, for in the Requiem Mass St. Michael is called upon to deliver the souls of the faithful "from the mouth of the lion, lest the jaws of the pit swallow them." This vivid image recalls the ancient Egyptian god Ammit, who was part lion and ate the souls of the sinful in the Great Judgment scene so often depicted in Egyptian art.

As in the case of the bear, however, what fascinated the medieval imagination most about the lion was the manner of its birth. It was believed that lion cubs were born dead and were given life by their father when he breathed on them. Here, the symbolic interpretation was simple: God the Father raised his Son, Jesus Christ, from the dead. It was also believed that lions slept with their eyes open, and again this was seen as God's watchfulness over his children.

Despite the Biblical and medieval symbolism of the lion as representa-

Lions are kings of beasts, and yet their pow'r
Is not to rule and govern, but devour.

Samuel Butler: *Miscellaneous Thoughts*

tive of Christ, no medieval cookbook recommended eating lion's flesh to become Christlike. Arab women, however, who are perhaps among the most suppressed females on the earth, used to feed their male children a piece of lion's heart to insure that the boys would grow up to be strong and manly. Here the women were making their own jailers fit.

Considering the lion's reputation as King of the Beasts, it is somewhat curious that according to medieval folklore he was afraid of creaking wheels, scorpions, fires, snake poison, and most of all the cock. Why the cock? In the cock he had the only serious rival to his kingship, since the cock also wore a crown when he announced the rising sun. In much literature and folklore the cock is also used as a symbol of the sun, and everyone believed there was only one sun in the universe.

Although the lion is a king and despot, he is tempered with gentleness and kindness. Royalty does not harm royalty in the lion's case; we know, however, how many human royal houses have filled cemeteries with each other's blood. The lion will not touch a human prince, or for that matter eat a woman or a child. In fact so kind and generous is the lion that if you behave properly, bowing to him, he will not harm you at all. Shakespeare in his bitter play *Troilus and Cressida* (V.3) has Troilus say, regarding the overkindness of lions:

> *Brother, you have a vice of mercy in you*
> *Which better fits a lion than a man.*

The lion's reputation for kindness extends back to an early, famous tale, generally known as *Androcles and the Lion*, variants of which are found in many collections such as Aesop, the *Gesta Romanorum,* and the Hindu *Katha Sarit Sagara.* Androcles, a runaway slave, fled into the forest to escape his master. As he was wandering about he came upon a moaning lion. At first Androcles turned to flee, but finding that the lion did not pursue him, he turned back and went up to him. As Androcles came near, the lion put out his paw, which was all swollen and bleeding. Androcles found that a huge thorn had pierced it and was causing the lion much pain. He pulled out the thorn and bound up the paw. When he had done this, the lion got up and licked Androcles like a pet dog. The lion then took the runaway slave to his cave and brought him meat every day.

But one day both Androcles and the lion were captured. The slave was sentenced to be thrown to the lions. When he was cast out into the arena, he was met by his lion friend, who defended him against the other lions. The crowd was so amazed that both Androcles and the lion were given their freedom.

This tale has been the source of numerous saint legends. St. Jerome, for example, is reported to have removed the thorn from a lion's paw, which is why he is always painted with a lion close by. And the tale supplied Shaw with the crux of his play *Androcles and the Lion,* which really has very little to do with lions but a lot to do with Christian hypocrisy.

The ancient pagan tale of Androcles and the Christian legend of St. Jerome might seem far-fetched at first, but a story is told of Sir George Davis, English consul at Florence at the beginning of the nineteenth century, that is quite similar. Sir George went to visit the Duke of Tuscany's lions. One of the lions could not be tamed, but as soon as it saw Sir George, it showed every sign of joy. Sir George entered the cage and the lion licked his face and wagged its tail. Later the consul said it was a lion he had brought up but sold when it became too big and dangerous.

While Sir George's tale might be as true as Androcles' and St. Jerome's, the Lion Sermon preached every year in October at St. Katharine Cree Church in London is quite real. It commemorates the "wonderful escape" of Sir John Gayer from a lion he met in the desert while traveling in Turkish dominions. Sir John was Lord Mayor of London in 1646!

COYOTE AND HYENA

A coyote had outwitted a bison for a cow and was quite proud of himself. He decided to take a little nap before eating his prize. While he slept he dreamed that some wolves came and ate the cow. When he awoke he found nothing but cow bones were left on the ground.

"Who dared do this!" he cried to the silent prairie, but no one answered.

Trying to make the best of it, the coyote decided he would eat the marrow of the bones, but he needed a sharp stone to get it out. While he was searching for the stone a badger came along and sucked out the bone marrow. When the coyote returned, he flew into a rage.

"Then I'll beat the bones to a powder," he decided.

But the bones scattered all over when he tried to pulverize them with a stone. The frustrated coyote then noticed some crows flying overhead.

"Peck at the bones so they become powder," he yelled to them, "then I'll give you half."

The crows agreed but said they needed a spoon. So the coyote went off to find a spoon, and while he was gone, the crows pecked all the bones and ate the powder. When the coyote returned, the crows flew overhead, crying: "Stupid! Stupid!" The coyote threw the spoon at them and fled, ashamed that he had been shown to be such a fool.

Although we may feel some sympathy for the coyote in this American Indian moralistic tale, we have to remember that the coyote tricked the bison to get the cow in the first place. The tale was used by the American Indians to instill in their children a code of behavior by showing that the coyote was punished for his greed.

An even stronger punishment is meted out to the coyote in another American Indian tale that tells how an entire coyote family was killed by a porcupine because one of its members cheated the porcupine out of some buffalo meat. We might feel that the price paid for the misdeed far exceeds the worth of the meat until we realize that buffalo meat was the mainstay of many an Indian diet.

Both tales stress that the coyote was an unsuccessful trickster, since he did not achieve his ends. In two American Indian creation myths, however, the coyote's role is rather more impressive. In one, the animal prevented Kodoyanpe, the Creator, from turning some wooden dummies into animals. In anger Kodoyanpe left, and the coyote took the wooden dummies, planted them—and Indians sprout up. Another tale has the coyote plant some bird feathers that sprouted into men. This motif is similar to the Greek legend of Cadmus, who sowed dragon's teeth from which men sprang up.

In spite of greediness and stupidity, then, the coyote is still a rather enviable animal, which cannot be said for the hyena. This doglike animal, with a large head and forequarters but weak hindquarters, appears in European and African myth as a demonic being.

The medieval concept of the hyena is clearly set out in *Le Trésor* by Brunetto Latini, the teacher and friend of Dante. (Friend or not, Dante placed the man in hell because of his homosexual proclivities.) Latini's work, written in French—a language he considered "most delectable"—is an encyclopedic work on history, natural science, ethics, rhetoric, and politics. His entry for the hyena runs as follows:

The hyena is sometimes male and sometimes female. It lives in cemeteries and eats the corpses of the dead; its spine is so stiff that it can't bend its body unless it turns completely around. It can imitate the sound of human voices, and often fools men and dogs, who come to it and are devoured.

Many say it has in its eyes a stone that if it were put under a man's

tongue it would enable him to see into the future. If the hyena casts
a shadow, whatever is under the shadow will become transfixed and
not be able to move. It accomplishes this through some form of
magic spells.

In Ethiopia the hyena copulates with a lion and produces the
Crocote, which has no teeth or gums in its mouth, but all its teeth
are one piece, like a box lid.

This fantastic entry cannot be ascribed just to flights of the medieval mind, since many of the superstitions mentioned throughout Latini's work date back to the time of Aristotle. The ancients believed the hyena changed its sex and added that if you caught the animal while it was male and castrated it, you could use its testicles to make a fine powder which would cure cramps. This cure was recommended by Dioscorides, a Greek physician of the first century, in his book on medicine. Not found in Dioscorides' book, but held as a general remedy against sterility, was hyena sinew mixed with frankincense and dropped into liquid.

In an African folktale the hyena and the hare agreed to kill their mothers and eat them, since there was no food available. The hyena, good to his word, killed his mother, prepared her body for dinner, and the two animals made a feast of her. When the hare's turn came to slay his mother for the next day's dinner, he decided not to go through with the plan. His action so enraged the hyena that he went to the hare's mother and murdered her himself.

We are not told whether the hare, faced with the *fait accompli* of his mother prepared for a tasty meal, changed his mind again and joined in the dinner. Certainly the moral question is worthy of an Aristotle or an Aquinas.

WOLF

One day Zeus decided to visit Arcadia, which was ruled by King Lycaon who had fifty children. The god, taking on the form of a traveler, left his heavenly home and went to the palace. A great feast was held for him, since some of the people said they recognized Zeus himself in the form of the traveler. Lycaon, however, was not convinced that the old man was the god and decided to test the issue. He went to the room of his grandson Arcas, the son of Callisto and Zeus, and murdered him. Then he prepared a meal from the body of Arcas for the god.

When the dish was presented to Zeus, he overturned the table and destroyed the house with a thunderbolt, transforming the king into a ravening wolf as punishment for his cannibalism. Later Arcas was restored to life by the god.

The Greeks probably invented this tale of Zeus' anger to protest human sacrifices at a time when such practices were common among them. Robert Graves in *The Greek Myths* says there was a shrine to Zeus at Mount Lycaeus where human sacrifices, as well as cannibalistic feasting, were the usual ritual. After the victim was eaten the worshipers were turned into wolves. Arcadian Zeus, Graves postulates, was originally a rain-making sacred king in the service of the divine she-wolf, the moon.

Lycaon's punishment and his werewolf nature fascinated European folk-lore for centuries. In sixteenth-century France there was an epidemic of werewolf stories and executions. One French tale of the time relates how a noblewoman was transformed into a *loup-garou*, or werewolf. She then attacked her gamekeeper, who in the ensuing struggle cut off one of her paws. When the gamekeeper brought the paw to the lord of the manor, it had transformed itself back into a human hand. The nobleman recognized the hand as that of his wife by the ancestral ring on one of the fingers.

The most notorious of the French werewolves of the period was Gilles Garnier. He was reported to have murdered children and eaten their raw flesh. Sometimes he was seen in human shape, sometimes as the werewolf.

When the werewolf phenomenon reached the theologians, they debated whether the animal was a true wolf, a wolf possessed by a demon, or an illusion. One whole chapter of the classic witchcraft manual *The Malleus Maleficarum,* or *The Hammer of Witches* (which has more detailed information on witches than one would really care to know), never settles the issue. The two Dominican authors contend that werewolves are true wolves possessed by devils, but then, they go on, the werewolves might also be illusions caused by devils.

King James I of England, noted paradoxically for his male favorites and the Authorized Version of the Bible, did not hedge on the question at all. An avid believer in witchcraft, the clever king nevertheless made the observation that some "men have thought themselves verrie woolfes" through "an superabundance of melancholy." A modern Freudian, Ernest Jones, in dealing with the same subject classifies the victims as cases of cannibalism and necrophilia, since the werewolf seeks to devour human flesh.

Freudian interest in werewolves is nowhere so strong as Hollywood's fascination with the subject. Hollywood's solution to the transformation was a good make-up department and a full moon. The full moon motif derives in part from a gruesome tale of destruction and renewal in Scandinavian mythology. The tale tells how the Managram, or Moon's Dog, a gigantic wolf, will drink the blood of the dead, swallow the moon, and cover the sky with blood to announce the end of the world.

The Moon Dog is probably a poetic description of an eclipse, which mythology often connected with the wolf, since the creature howled at night when the moon was up. In a Yugoslavian tale of the thirteenth century the werewolf Vukodlak devoured the moon, causing an eclipse.

Each European area has developed its own signs to identify a werewolf. In Sicilian folklore a man whose eyebrows meet is considered a werewolf. Even in Denmark today this superstition is current. In Slavic mythology a child born feet first or with teeth will become a werewolf. In other countries a child born on Christmas Day becomes a werewolf because it is an insult to God to be born on Christ's birthday.

As recently as 1720 a werewolf was executed in Mozart's native city of Salzburg. (No less could be expected from a city that did not appreciate Mozart's genius.) Not only was the suspected werewolf hanged and mutilated, its body was also burned, for if not completely destroyed it would return as a vampire, causing even more havoc.

Yet even a "fallen" wolf had a chance of redemption, according to Christian folklore, as one tale contained in Helen Waddell's *Beasts and Saints* clearly indicates.

A hermit daily fed a she-wolf. One day while the hermit was away and unable to feed her, the she-wolf stole some of his bread. When the man returned, he realized what had happened. Days passed, seven to be exact, before the she-wolf came and with her eyes asked forgiveness for what she had done.

The writer of this tale concludes with the touching line: "Consider, I pray you, in this example of it the power of Christ, with whom brute beast is wise, and every savage creature gentle."

But to most readers the best-known of this type of tale is probably the one of St. Francis and the wolf of Gubbino. Certainly this saint has been identified in the popular imagination with his love for animals. The wolf story is included in *The Little Flowers of St. Francis*, a collection of tales and legends about the saint and his companions.

During the Middle Ages it was not uncommon for wolves to come down from the mountains seeking food, especially in times of famine, and one such wolf was devastating the town of Gubbino. Francis, resolving to help the townspeople, went out with his disciples to meet the wolf. They drew back, however, and only Francis proceeded. Seeing himself surrounded by people, the wolf ran toward Francis with his jaws wide open. The saint, making the sign of the cross, said: "Come here, brother wolf. I command you, in the name of Christ, neither to hurt me nor anyone else."

No sooner had the saint finished than the wolf closed his jaws, stopped running, and lay down at the saint's feet as meek as a lamb. Francis then made a pact with the wolf in which he promised to have the people feed the animal if the wolf would no longer molest them. The wolf showed his approval by giving his paw to the saint. For two years the animal lived on in the town and was known by the people as Fra Lupo, or Brother Wolf.

Both these Christian tales present the wolf as "fallen" from grace but "redeemable." This idea of a guilt-ridden animal is entirely missing from the American Indian approach to the beast. In a tale of the East Cree Indians the wolf was responsible for the creation of the earth, in direct contrast with the Scandinavian myth in which the wolf announced the earth's destruction.

One day, according to the Indian tale, Trickster Wisagatcak built a dam across a creek in order to trap the giant beaver. When the beaver approached him at nightfall, Trickster was ready. A muskrat, however, bit Trickster and so Trickster missed his target. The next day he took down the dam. The other beavers, in order to get revenge, let the water flow until the entire land was covered and there was no earth. For two weeks the waters rose. The muskrat dove down to see how deep the water was and drowned. A raven went out and found no land. Finally Wisagatcak called the wolf for help. The wolf ran round and round a raft with a ball of moss in his mouth. The ball of moss grew and earth formed on it. When he put it down, all the animals danced around, singing powerful spells. The earth grew and grew, spreading over the raft; it went on growing until it made the whole world.

Yahweh God was looking out on his whole creation and quite pleased with it when the Angel of Death approached his throne.

"Yahweh," said the Angel of Death, "you have not yet let me kill any creature. Everything still lives. May I please have permission to kill two of every living creature?"

"Yes," replied Yahweh, "but you may not kill any of them before their allotted time."

So with Yahweh's approval the Angel of Death descended to earth and set about murdering two of every creature. Eventually he came upon two foxes, both of whom were weeping.

"You have killed our mother and father," they cried together.

The Angel of Death insisted he had not killed any foxes, but the two insisted all the more.

"Come," they said to the Angel of Death, "and we will show you the bodies of our dead parents."

The Angel of Death accompanied the two to the water's edge. Upon arriving there they leaned over the edge and pointed to their own reflections.

"There are our parents! Now don't touch us, for you have promised Yahweh not to kill anyone before his time."

The Angel of Death, fooled by the cunning foxes, let them escape.

This Jewish folktale exemplifies one of the most persistent motifs in folklore: the cunningness of the fox in outsmarting other creatures. This reputation, however, is not founded on natural lore. The animal is no craftier than most other beasts of prey. Yet for thousands of years the fox has been the symbol of shrewdness and deceit.

Shrewdness is always admired by people even if their society or culture says it is immoral. This accounts for the extreme popularity of the fox in folklore and literature. The medieval French evolved an entire beast-epic, the *Roman de Renart*, tracing the adventures of Renard the Fox, and other cultures have followed. An English version was published by Caxton in the fifteenth century, while both Goethe and John Masefield wrote long narrative poems on the adventures of Renard. Igor Stravinsky's opera-ballet *Renard* also treats the subject.

One typical episode from the medieval French work makes clear that whenever the fox gains over his adversaries, it is through exploiting some weakness of theirs, such as greed, vanity, or gluttony.

In the episode a bear was sent out to bring the fox to court to answer numerous charges made against him by other animals. When the bear arrived at the fox's home, the fox spoke sweetly, telling the bear there was a place where he could eat all the honey he wanted. The bear, forgetting his mission and greedy for the honey, decided to follow the fox to the secret place. Through the fox's scheming the bear was caught in the wedges of a tree trunk as he sought the honey. To add to the bear's misery, the fox taunted him.

"Is the honey good, uncle? Don't eat too much or else you'll stuff yourself and won't be able to go to court with me!"

Finally the landowner came—a priest, accompanied by some others. They beat the bear almost to death, but he managed to flee, minus his ears and most of his skin.

This sadistic episode leaves the fox completely victorious. Sometimes, however, he does not come out so well. Perhaps the best example of this is in the Nun's Priest's Tale from Chaucer's *The Canterbury Tales*.

It is impossible in a short resume of the tale to capture the flavor of Chaucer's verse and wit. Since the complete tale is easily available, a quick summary of the main story line will do. Russel the fox had been eyeing Chanticleer the cock and his whole harem, among them the hen Pertelote. Finally Russel made his move. He persuaded Chanticleer to sing, since he

It is the animal with the big tail, a tail many
yards long and like a fox's brush ... the tail is
constantly being flung this way and that.

Franz Kafka: *Dearest Father*

sang so well. Chanticleer, moved by the false flattery, stood up on his toes, stretched out his neck, closed his eyes, and began to sing. In no time the fox had grabbed Chanticleer and fled the barnyard. The entire community of barn animals became hysterical. The wives and friends lamented and cried, calling on one another to help catch up with the fox. Chanticleer, his tail stuck in the fox's mouth, spoke to him.

"Sir, if I were you I would say to them, as God is my witness, 'Turn back, you fools, it's no use. Now that I'm in the forest the cock will be mine to eat!' "

"That's just what I'll do," said the fox. But no sooner did he speak the few words than Chanticleer broke loose and fled to the top of a tree. The fox tried again through flattery to get Chanticleer down, but this time the cock was too smart to be fooled.

How did the fox, supposedly so clever, get taken in by such an obvious ploy? The answer lies in the symbolic roles of the animals of Chaucer's tale.

The fox often represents the night and the cock, the day, in much mythology. The persistence of this symbolism is so strong that the modern Czech composer Leoš Janáček, basing his opera *Cunning Little Vixen* on a fox tale, finally has the vixen meet her end through a chicken peddler. Murder by the cock secondhand, but murder nevertheless. Whether Chaucer intentionally used mythological symbolism in his tale of the fox and the cock, or merely employed the situation for its satirical qualities, is an interesting question, for no direct source is known for the tale. Certainly in Chaucer's day there were collections in circulation of Greek and Latin fables of the fox and the cock. The poet was a learned and well-read man, though he wore his learning lightly and naturally—a gift not always true of great poets (Milton, for instance, always makes us so immediately aware of his great knowledge). Aesop's fables contain examples in which the fox gets the worst of the deal, as in Chaucer's tale, although the predominant theme in Aesop and other collections is one of the fox's craftiness and final victory over a host of animals.

In Dante's *Inferno* the spirit of Guido da Montefeltro, a famous warrior and leader of the Ghibellines, a political faction in Florence, says that his deeds were not those of a lion, but of a fox. He used crafty, secretive ways to achieve his ends. While Dante places Montefeltro in hell, Machiavelli in *The Prince* advises rulers to imitate two animals: the lion and the fox. The strength of the lion, Machiavelli says, is not sufficient for a ruler; he must also have the deceit of the fox.

The Oriental mind views the fox somewhat differently. Japanese and Chinese lore abounds with stories of fox transformations—women turned into foxes or foxes into women. While the werewolf in European myth is diabolical, the Oriental fox-woman is usually a beneficent spirit. One eighth-century classic tale, *The Fox Fairy*, by the Chinese writer Shên Chi-chi, is concerned with a lovely fox-spirit that brought only good luck to her lover, but disaster upon herself. One day, Chêng, a soldier, came upon three women walking on the road and became fascinated by one of them, Miss Jên. He spoke with her and she invited him to spend the evening in her palace, but she told him he must leave early the next day. Chêng left early the next morning before the gates to the city were opened. He spent the time talking to a baker who had a shop just outside the city gates. When he asked the baker who owned the palace in the forest, the baker replied,

"No one," since it was in ruins. Chêng then realized that he had been tricked by a fox-maiden. Yet when he saw her again, he entered into a liaison with her, they set up house, and both were quite happy. Miss Jên brought him good luck, advising him to buy a certain house and resell it at a large profit. He did what she told him and made considerable money.

Finally Chêng asked Miss Jên to travel with him to his new military post, but she refused, saying a fortuneteller had told her she would meet an ill end. He insisted, and she in her love for him agreed. As they proceeded along the road, a dog appeared and rushed after the maiden, who suddenly turned into a vixen. The chase lasted for about a mile until the vixen was finally caught and torn to pieces by the dog.

In Oriental tales the appearance of a dog always forces the fox-maiden into revealing her nature. Also, if a fox-maiden looks into water, only her fox features will be reflected. In Japanese folklore a fox-maiden can be recognized by a spurt of flame flickering over her human head.

The sexual aspect of the fox, recognized by the Chinese, is also evident in Japanese art and literature. In one four-panel Japanese erotic art work, for instance, some rich merchants are shown engaged in various sexual activities with different women. In the next panel (much as in a cartoon strip) the women have turned into vixens and the men into peasants.

The sexual connotations of the fox are explored by D. H. Lawrence in his short novel *The Fox*, but here the animal stands for male sexuality. Whether or not one finds the characters of Lawrence's novella believable depends a good deal on whether one can accept his fiction as a whole. He so often overloads his gun, so to speak, that when he shoots, the victim is smashed beyond interest. A much more enjoyable book is David Garnett's novel of the early 1920s *Lady into Fox*.

Leaving the sexual symbolism of the fox aside, we find the fox also serves another function in mythology. The Japanese worship a fox-goddess Inari as the rice-spirit. In *The Golden Bough* Frazer names the fox as one of the animals symbolic of the corn- or wheat-spirit. The origin of the connection between wheat fields and the fox is perhaps shown in the Biblical story of Samson (Judges 13–16).

When Samson was denied his life, he vented his anger on the Philistines by catching three hundred foxes, tying them together in pairs and putting a torch between each pair of tails. He then set fire to the torches and let them loose. The foxes burned up the sheaves of wheat and the standing corn, as well as the grapevines and the olive trees.

There is considerable debate among Bible scholars about what the fox episode means. One theory holds that Samson is a solar hero, his action representing the scorching sun. Another possibility is that the tale as narrated in Judges is a distorted remembrance of an ancient rite to remove mildew from crops, such as the one mentioned by Ovid, where it was customary to send foxes into the fields to remove mildew.

Yet Samson's action may have been just a clever stratagem comparable to that of Hannibal. Livy in *A History of Rome* tells how Hannibal, being blocked by the Romans, "caused bundles of rods and dry twigs to be tied fast on the horns of oxen" and then drove them up the Alpine mountains and over the passes. When the Romans saw the flames, they "concluded they were surrounded, and quitted their post. . . ." (As in so much Biblical criticism, it is up to the reader to decide which theory he accepts.)

Perhaps the most baffling Biblical verses on foxes are contained in the erotic love poem The Song of Solomon (2:15):

> *Take us the foxes,*
> *the little foxes,*
> *that spoil the vines;*
> *for our vines have tender grapes.*

Lillian Hellman, taking her cue from the verse, used the second line as the title of her well-known drama of rapaciousness, although this interpretation of the verse does not receive general acceptance among Bible scholars. If the text refers to a fertility rite, as some commentators believe, the exact nature of the rite eludes them. Perhaps the fox has some sexual connotation in The Song of Solomon as it does in Chinese and Japanese mythology.

What would be the final verdict of mythology on the fox? For the Western world we can echo the line of one fox's victim, who cried out: "Why, the whole world knows he is a murderer, a vagabond, and a thief. He doesn't love any creature!" Yet an Oriental would certainly find objection to this characterization of the fox. Surely an animal that can show the love Miss Jên displays in the Chinese tale, sacrificing her life for her lover's wish, deserves a better reputation.

DOG

Cerberus, a savage bronze-colored dog with fifty heads, was the guardian of the Underworld in Greek mythology. He would eat those spirits who tried to flee the dismal abode. The last and most difficult of Heracles' Twelve Labors was to bring the monster-dog back from the Underworld and present him to King Eurystheus. The king had hoped that Heracles would be killed in the venture, since he was a lifelong foe of the hero.

Two gods, Hermes and Athene (she always looked after the hero), came along with Heracles to help him in the task. When the party boarded Charon's boat to cross over the river of death, the ferryman was so frightened by Heracles' scowl he did not ask any questions. As a result Charon was punished by Hades, king of the Underworld, who chained him for a year. There is no mention who ferried the dead across the river in his absence.

Heracles proceeded to the throne room of the king and demanded Cerberus from the god.

"He is yours," replied Hades, "if you can capture him without the use of clubs or arrows."

Undaunted, Heracles went to where Cerberus was chained and he grabbed the beast by the throat. The monster's heads tried one after the other to attack him, but to no avail. Heracles then choked the dog into submission.

Having mastered the animal, Heracles made his way to the upper world and to King Eurystheus, who of course expected never to see Heracles again. When the king was presented with the beast, who snarled and glared at him, he jumped into a large jar and died of fright. Heracles, his task completed, returned Cerberus to Hades.

Heracles was not the only hero to visit the Underworld and meet Cerberus. Aeneas, the hero of Virgil's epic poem *The Aeneid*, also had a run-in with the beast. His dealings, however, were less heroic but cleverer. Aeneas was accompanied by the Cumaean Sybil, a prophetess. When she saw Cerberus ready to spring at her hero, she threw him a honeycake which it gobbled up. The cake was drugged, the beast fell asleep, and Aeneas easily passed him. Virgil disliked violence of any sort (Napoleon said Virgil's battle scenes were all wrong), so he often has his hero guided and protected by Venus.

Later writers used Cerberus for satirical purposes. Lucian, the second-century Greek writer, in one of his *Dialogues of the Dead* reports a meeting between the cynic philosopher Menippus and Cerberus in hell.

"Cerberus," Menippus said, "I'm a kind of cousin of yours, you know— they also call me a dog. [Cynic is derived from the Greek word for dog.] Tell me, how did Socrates behave when he came down here? I suppose, as you're a divinity, you can talk as well as bark."

"When he was some way off," replied the dog, "Socrates came on with a perfectly unmoved countenance, appearing to have no dread at all of death. But then he got within the archway of the Shades, and saw the gloom and darkness. Since he took his time, I had to bite him on the foot to help the hemlock along. Then he began to cry like a baby. He cried about his family and friends."

"So he was but a sophist after all," Menippus said with a smile. "He had no true contempt for death?"

"No," replied Cerberus. "When he saw it must come, he prepared himself. He said since he had to die, it was better to die well as an example to his friends. I could tell you lots of stories of those who die bravely, but break down once they come here in sight of all the misery."

"How did I behave?"

"You were one of the best," Cerberus said. "You laughed all the way."

Menippus must have been a brave man to laugh at the many-headed

Cerberus, but by the time Lucian wrote his satire the dog's fifty heads had been reduced to a mere three. The early Greek writer Hesiod says the animal had fifty, but Virgil and Ovid only cite three. This reduction might have been the result of the beast's later connection with Hecate, the goddess of death, who was often portrayed as a three-headed monster, perhaps signifying the Past, Present, and Future.

Although the dog's connection with Hecate is tenuous, he was definitely associated with the Great Mother-Goddess. The male votaries of the goddess dressed in women's clothing and were called *kalabim*, or dogs.

Cerberus' role in Greek and Roman myth has numerous counterparts in other European mythologies. In the North, for instance, the blood-spattered demon-dog Garmr watched over the house of the dead, ready to fight the gods at the end of the world. In many European tales the souls of the damned are hunted to the Northern Hell by a pack of hounds. César Franck, the nineteenth-century Belgian composer, wrote a symphonic poem *Le Chasseur maudit*, or *The Accursed Huntsman*, based on the legend of a man who was pursued by hounds for hunting on the Sabbath.

Demon-dogs are also found in Asian and South American tales and legends. The Buddhists have dogs that inflict punishment in hell, while the Hindu god of death, Yama, has two dogs that are sent out to bring back wandering souls. In Middle American mythology a red dog was sacrificed by the Aztecs to carry the soul of a dead king across a deep stream or to announce his arrival in the other world.

The dog is referred to some forty-one times in the Bible. Deuteronomy 23:18 sums up the Hebrew attitude: "Thou shalt not bring the hire of a whore, or the price of a dog, into the house of the Lord thy God for any vow: for even both these are abomination unto the Lord thy God."

The hatred of dogs perhaps comes from the fact that the animals ran in packs throughout many Eastern cities, howling, snarling, and scavenging—making them unclean in the eyes of the Hebrews. However, in the Book of Tobit (5:16) in the Old Testament Apocrypha there is a mention of Tobit's dog. Moslem legend goes so far as to put Tobit's dog in heaven, along with Borak, the horse of the Prophet, Balaam's ass, and Kasmir, the dog of the Seven Sleepers. This Christian legend of Kasmir, adapted by the Moslems, is an early expression of the "man's best friend" ideal.

Seven youths hid in a cave to escape persecution and fell asleep for two hundred years. When they awoke, one of them went into the city to get provisions. When he returned, they all fell asleep again until eventually they were admitted into heaven. During the entire time their dog Kasmir waited outside the cave—not eating or drinking, or even sleeping.

Kasmir is one of many dogs of literature and legend noted for faithfulness. One Roman tale tells how a dog guarded the body of its murdered master when enemy troops came to decapitate the man to insure his spirit would not come back to plague them. The dog howled and snarled until it became necessary for the soldiers to subdue the animal; then they could carry out this final atrocity.

There are also many ancient and modern tales where a dog helps to solve a crime. Plutarch reports the tale of how King Pyrrhus came upon a dog on the road, guarding the body of a dead man. The dog was taken back to the palace by the king, fed, and made comfortable. One day while the king was reviewing troops, the dog began to growl and bark at some soldiers. The men were arrested, questioned, and found guilty of the murder of the dog's master. Medieval legend tells of the case of Aubry of Montdidier, who was murdered in 1371. His dog Dragon always snarled and went for the throat of a man named Richard of Macaire. Years later Richard was condemned to judicial combat with the dog. He lost, and with his dying breath Richard admitted he had killed Aubry.

Partly because of such Christian legends the dog often became a symbol of conscience. Yet despite faithfulness and identification with moral attributes, the dog was also associated with the devil. One Christian tale tells of a woman whose only son was tormented by the devil. When the devil entered into him, the lad began to bite anyone who came near. If no one were near enough to bite, he would bite himself. As a result the boy's entire body was covered with wounds. The distraught mother, upon hearing that a child named Jesus could cure persons possessed, went to Mary, the mother of Jesus, and begged for help. While the two women were talking, the possessed boy left the house and went to sit next to the boy Jesus. As soon as Jesus touched the boy, the devil jumped out of the boy's mouth in the form of a mad dog. The boy's name, the tale informs us, was Judas Iscariot.

Yet, the dog's beneficent, godlike nature is also stressed in its identification with Christ. Perhaps the best-known poem on this aspect is Francis Thompson's great ode, *The Hound of Heaven*. This rich and sensuous poem, inspired by seventeenth-century English Baroque poetry, details a soul's flight from God and God's unrelenting, houndlike pursuit.

Walt Disney's cartoon creation, Pluto, combines the beneficent aspect of the dog with a demonic name, since Pluto is the Latin form of Hades, the god of the Underworld, whose dog was Cerberus.

The popularity of cartoon dogs such as Pluto and Snoopy of "Peanuts" fame would have puzzled the seventeenth-century French philosopher René Descartes, who said a dog was nothing but a machine without feeling or emotion. Madame de Sévigné, a sensitive lady of the time, replied: "Machines which love, which prefer one person to another, machines which are jealous . . . come now! Descartes never thought to make us believe that!"

COW AND BULL

In the beginning of time there lived a cow, Audhumla, or Audhubla, formed from the melting ice-drops. Her breath was sweet but her milk bitter. She lived all by herself on a frosty, misty plain, where there was nothing to be seen but heaps of snow and ice. Far away to the North was night, and to the South day, but all around Audhumla lay a cold, gray twilight. From out of the dark North a giant, Ymir, came and lay down upon the ice near Audhumla.

"Let me drink your milk," the giant said to the cow. And though her milk was bitter, Ymir liked it.

After some time Audhumla looked around for something to eat, and she saw some grains of salt sprinkled over the ice. She licked the salt, breathing upon it, and long golden locks appeared out of the ice. Ymir was angry when he saw the glitter of the golden hair, but Audhumla licked the salt again, and the head of a man arose out of the ice. Now Ymir became angrier, but the cow continued to lick the salt until an entire man arose—a majestic figure, Buri, who was the father of Borr and grandfather of the great gods Odin, Vili, and Ve.

After the birth of the gods Ymir vowed to destroy all three, but they slew him instead. From Ymir's body they formed the world. His blood became the seas and lakes; his flesh the earth, his bones the mountains; his teeth, jaws, and broken bones the rocks and pebbles. From his skull the gods formed the dome of the sky, placing a dwarf to support each of its four corners. Then the gods created man and woman from two trees.

This Eddic creation myth from the North represents a rather constant motif in world mythology: the cow as symbol of fecundity and creation. In primitive Egyptian mythology, for example, the sky-moon-goddess Hathor was pictured in the form of a cow. Her name, which means "house of Horus," shows her to be a mother and fertility goddess, since she is both the mother and consort of the great god Ra. Hathor is at once loving and terrifying, for she is also mistress of the Underworld. When Ra punished man, he sent Hathor to perform the task, though she became so carried away by her mission that she nearly destroyed all of mankind. To stop the murder, the other gods finally made her drunk with beer. (Evidently, she became calm with alcohol.)

Often Hathor and the goddess Isis were confused in later Egyptian mythology, Isis assuming the role and symbols of Hathor. In turn Isis was identified by the Greeks with Io (who was turned into a heifer by Zeus) and with Aphrodite. The Romans identified her with Ceres and Venus (the Roman equivalents of Demeter and Aphrodite). The Isis cult lasted until well into the sixth century A.D. She was often sculpted or painted as a mother nursing a child, with the crescent moon as her symbol. Her iconographic setting was absorbed into the symbolism surrounding the Virgin Mary, who took on all the good attributes of the earlier goddesses, and none of their terrifying aspects.

The Moslems tell a tale of a childless Egyptian couple who envied the fruitfulness of their cow. Allah in his mercy let the cow speak to the couple. The cow told them that they had no son because Fate decreed that if they did, the son would be wicked. This news did not deter the couple, who still wished for a male child, so Allah granted their request. Their son was born, and he turned out to be the wicked Pharaoh who oppressed the children of Israel.

During their later flight from Egypt Yahweh accompanied the Israelites by signs, a cloud by day and a light by night. These signs, however, did not satisfy the people, and while Moses was away on Mount Sinai, they asked that Aaron make them a golden calf. Aaron collected all the golden ornaments that the Hebrews brought with them from Egypt, and he constructed a golden idol. The people worshiped the calf with fertility rites.

This scene is vividly painted by Tintoretto in his *Worship of the Golden Calf*, and depicted in Arnold Schönberg's opera *Moses and Aaron*. The theme has always given artists a license to display a sexual theme with the "sanction" of the Bible. DeMille often used this gimmick in his films.

The golden calf worshiped by the Hebrews resembles the worship of the bull Hap or Apis in Egypt. Hap was the sacred bull of Memphis and was believed to be the incarnation of the gods Ptah and Osiris. He was born of a virgin cow and was recognized by the markings that resembled eagle's wings on his back and forehead. Under his tongue was a hump in the shape of a scarab, another sacred Egyptian symbol. The bull was kept in a shrine facing East and fed for four months, when he was then taken with great ceremony down the Nile to Memphis, where sacrifices were made to him. Each year the animal's birthday was celebrated, but if he lived past his twenty-fifth year, he was drowned in a sacred cistern and mourned for seventy days. The Egyptians would then look for a replacement for the dead god, and the process would start all over again.

Bull worship was not confined in the East to the Egyptians and Hebrews. In ancient Persia the Supreme Bull was believed to cause the grass to grow. He was, like the Hebrew god, without any beginning or end, but existed before all time and for all time. In the Persian cult of the light-god Mithras, which spread throughout the Roman Empire from the second century A.D., Mithras would come and kill a bull at the end of the world so a new world could emerge. The ceremonies of the bull-slaying god took place in subterranean crypts where the worshiper went through numerous "transformations" until he or she was assured of resurrection at the end of the world. Mithras is usually represented as a young man in Oriental dress, stabbing a massive bull.

Some historians believe this cult had a great effect on the beliefs and teachings of early Christianity, though the question is by no means settled. Jung interprets the killing of a bull as the "triumph over the primitive animal passions of man. . . ." In the great epic poem *Gilgamesh,* for instance, the goddess Ishtar sent the bull of Heaven, Gudanna, to kill Gilgamesh because he refused to have sexual relations with her. But Gilgamesh and his friend Enkidu killed the celestial bull. In revenge Ishtar killed

Enkidu. Gudanna's counterpart in Hindu mythology is Arishta, a savage bull who attacked the god Krishna but was killed by the god.

Generally, however, in Hindu mythology the cow and the bull are beneficent. Nadi, the sacred bull of the god Siva in his gentle aspect as Pasupati —the Herdsman, Owner of Cattle, Lord of All Beasts—is honored throughout India. All the beasts of the field, wild and tame, belong to Siva, as do the souls of men, which are also called "cattle." Siva's role as herdsman resembles Christ's role as the Good Shepherd in Christian art, reflecting a time when civilization was basically pastoral. Until the early part of the last century, in special ceremonies in countries of Central and Eastern Europe, such sadistic practices as passing through fire and beating the bull for good luck were followed to make sure cattle were fertile, since so much depended on their ability to reproduce.

In Greek myth Zeus used the guise of a bull to seduce Europa, hoping thereby that his animal transformation would elude his ever-watchful wife Hera from detecting his adultery. Zeus fell in love with Europa, a Phoenician princess, and sent the god Hermes to lure the girl to the seashore, away from her companions. Zeus in the meantime assumed the appearance of a bull and stood by the sea. His color was snow white; his neck swelled with muscles; yet his appearance was one of gentleness and peace. Europa, seeing how lovely and unthreatening he was, approached and held out flowers to him. The bull then began to play with her, finally inducing Europa to sit on his back. He then moved slowly from the land toward the sea, and in no time bore her off over the waves, while she held onto his horn with one hand and his back with another. She and Zeus later had several sons.

The myth of Europa has been variously interpreted. Robert Graves in *The Greek Myths* sees the tale as recording an early Hellenic occupation of Crete. One nineteenth-century theory held that there was an actual person named Jupiter (one Roman form of Zeus' name) who abducted a princess named Europa in a ship; the figurehead of which was a bull. In Phoenician dialect the words "bull" and "ship" are quite similar and the two words were, according to this theory, confused in the transmission of the myth.

Whatever the true origin of the myth, it does contain strong sexual connotations. Renaissance painters were particularly attracted to portraying this aspect of the myth. Perhaps the most beautiful work is Titian's *Rape of*

Europa, where the girl's helplessness as well as sensuousness are magnificently conveyed through the use of color and rapid brush strokes, making the whole canvas vibrate with life.

The bull, however, was not associated only with Zeus in Greek mythology. The animal was symbolically killed by the followers of Dionysus during midsummer festivals in honor of the great god. Worshipers of the sea-god Poseidon sacrificed black bulls to him. The god was often addressed as "Father Poseidon, Lord of Bulls."

The rich mythological and religious connotations of the bull are reflected in much twentieth-century art and literature. Picasso's painting *Guernica,* depicting the horrors of an unprovoked German bombing attack on the small, undefended Basque town of Guernica, uses the bull as one of its central figures. Two days after the bombing the town fell to the Fascists under Franco. In the large canvas painted in blacks and grays stands a bull. According to the artist the bull symbolizes "brutality and darkness." Picasso's native Spain supplied him with enough knowledge of the animal and man's relation to it—epitomized by the bloody contest between the two in the bull ring. This theme also fascinated Ernest Hemingway. In many of his works the bull is seen as a brutal symbol of masculinity, not unlike the attitude of the Zulu warriors who drink the gall of bulls killed by the warriors with bare hands, while the boys eat the flesh to insure their strength and virility.

Yet in the well-known children's classic *Ferdinand the Bull* the hero, Ferdinand, a Spanish bull, prefers smelling flowers to fighting in the ring— something that certainly would have upset Hemingway. If the bull has lost some virility in the children's classic, the cow has retained all her mythological association. Elsie the cow, famous for decades as a symbol of Borden Inc., combines all the qualities of the goddesses Hathor, Isis, and Demeter. She gives life and health, all for the price of a quart of milk.

WILD BOAR, PIG, AND SOW

Oeneus, king of Calydon, sacrificed to the gods the first fruits of the earth every year. One year he forgot to offer Artemis her due, and in anger the moon-goddess sent a gigantic boar with fiery eyeballs, bristled back, and grunting nose to ravage his land. When the boar had so terrorized the subjects of the king that they feared to leave their homes, Oeneus asked other Greek cities for aid in destroying the beast. Many famous Greek heroes responded to the king's call.

With this hero-host of Greeks came an Arcadian maiden, Atalanta. Her appearance caused disagreement among the men. Ancaeus, the strongest next to Heracles, refused to hunt with her. Oeneus' son Meleager defended Atalanta's right to be there. Meleager had fallen in love with her almost on sight, but she had sworn never to marry after an oracle told her it would lead to disaster.

The hunt was about to begin when two centaurs, always on the prowl for some maidens to seduce, spied Atalanta and tried to rape her. But this maiden was not passive and in no time the centaurs lay dead, shot through with her arrows. The hunting party finally approached the watery bed where the boar lay. As it was flushed from it hiding place, each hero shot at the animal. The boar charged, killing two hunters. Atalanta shot an arrow that sank beneath the boar's ear. Ancaeus sneered at Atalanta.

"That is no way to hunt," he cried.

He swung his ax at the boar as it charged again, but through a miscalculation, the next moment he lay castrated and disembowled. Meleager then stepped in and killed the boar.

The prize—the boar's head and skin— went to Atalanta, since her arrow had shed the first blood. Two of Meleager's brothers objected to this award (they were not in love with Atalanta), and a fight ensued in which both brothers were killed by Meleager. When their mother heard what had happened, she vowed vengeance on her son.

At Meleager's birth his mother had been told that he would die when a log then on the fire was burned up. She had therefore removed the log and hid it. Now in her anger at the death of her other two sons, she removed the log from the chest and threw it on the fire. Meleager, feeling intense pain and not knowing the cause, soon died, his only lament being that he did not die a hero's death. Eventually Atalanta married. She met her death, just as foretold by the oracle, for having sexual relations with her husband in a sacred temple.

The Calydonian Boar Hunt, as the episode is usually called in Greek mythology, was extremely popular with ancient writers, not only for the blood-and-thunder elements of the hunt, but for its romantic interest as well. Ovid, the great romantic Latin poet, dwells on these elements in his telling of the myth, which supplied our source. Homer, more down to earth, says a war ensued between the Calydonians and their hostile neighbors the Curetes, who had joined the hunt. In one telling of the myth Meleager was granted his wish to die in battle instead of through his mother's witchcraft.

Certain elements in the tale, however, are constant in all the accounts: the ravaging boar, a young man castrated (Ancaeus), and a goddess. The boar sent to Calydon was sacred to Artemis. The boar's curved moon-shaped tusk made the animal an ideal symbol of the moon-goddess.

Other goddesses were identified with a white sow, such as the Egyptian Isis and the Greek goddess Demeter, who was often shown with a pig at her feet or in her arms. The Tibetan goddess Vajravareh, or Wanderer of the Air, also had the mark of the wild sow upon her. The identity of the sow with goddesses has made some Jungians interpret the pig symbol as that of the Great Mother-Goddess: all that is fertile, rich and open.

These Mother-Goddesses usually have young lover-consorts who die and are reborn, symbols of the annual cycle of the seasons and crops. Attis, an Asiatic divinity and the handsome consort of the goddess Cybele, was killed by a boar, although in one version of his death he castrated himself under a tree and bled to death from it. The story of Attis, however, is not as well known as that of Adonis, another young lover of a Mother-Goddess.

Adonis, or Lord (when the Greeks assimilated the Asiatic divinity they turned his title into a proper name), was loved by Aphrodite, whose cult originated in Asia as the Great Mother-Goddess. Adonis was the son of an incestuous union of a daughter and father. When the father realized that he had had intercourse with his daughter while he was drunk (she had not objected; being under a curse, she had in fact encouraged him), he was about to kill her when Aphrodite changed the poor girl into a myrrh tree. Before she was transformed, however, the girl gave birth to a handsome baby boy. Aphrodite put the infant in a chest and entrusted it to the goddess of the Underworld, Persephone. This goddess, curious to know what was in the chest, eventually opened it, and upon seeing the boy, fell in love with him. The two goddesses then fought for possession of the youth, who had by this time obviously reached puberty and had considerable attractions.

Finally the matter was brought before the Muse Calliope. In a very reasonable manner she decided that Adonis would spend one-third of the year with Persephone, one-third with Aphrodite, and one-third he would have free to himself. Calliope realized that the much-used boy needed a rest from the devouring goddesses. Aphrodite, greedy with sexual desire, cheated Persephone by wearing a magic girdle that made her irresistible to men. Adonis could not leave this goddess of love, and his obligation to Persephone was left unfulfilled. The goddess of the Underworld was naturally angry and went to Ares, the husband of Aphrodite, and told him that his wife was in love with a pretty youth and was spending all her time with him. Ares, the war-god, hated the idea of what he thought was an effeminate man making love to his wife. Taking the form of one of his sacred animals, the boar, Ares attacked Adonis when he was hunting and killed the youth.

Adonis' castration-death by the boar formed an elaborate part of the ritual surrounding the god. His cult was widely practiced in western Asia

and in certain Greek islands. Yearly his death and resurrection were celebrated with wailing and lamentation. Bion's poem *Lament for Adonis,*
written in the third-century B.C., was probably intended for one of the
spring festivals of the god. Images of Adonis dressed as a corpse were
carried in procession and then thrown into the sea. (The sea gave birth to
Aphrodite and is considered a symbol of female life-giving powers.) In
Alexandria images of Aphrodite and Adonis were shown on two couches
surrounded by fruits and cakes. On one day the marriage of the god and
goddess was celebrated; on the next day, his death, and later his rebirth.

These ceremonies were absorbed by Christianity. Often during Holy
Week a statue of the dead Christ is laid out on the side altar, with weeping
angels attending him. His battered blood-stained body is there until Holy
Saturday, when it is removed, and next day a plaster statue of the Resur-
rected Christ put in its place. The death and resurrection of Adonis and
Christ are both classic examples of the springtime "dying and reviving god,"
as Frazer points out in *The Golden Bough.*

Other male deities besides the handsome Adonis, Attis, and Ares
were associated with the boar or pig. Osiris, the Egyptian god of the dead
and afterlife, had a pig sacrificed to him on the anniversary of his death.

Osiris was murdered by his brother Set (who was often pictured with a
pig's head and a flint knife, symbols of dismemberment and death). In the
Egyptian tale Osiris was castrated, and his penis thrown into the sea and
eaten by a fish. It was the one part of his dismembered body that his wife-
sister Isis could not recover.

If we wish to be logical, how can the pig be a symbol both of the god
Osiris and of his killer Set? Frazer postulates an answer:

> *The animal, which at first has been slain in the character of the god,*
> *comes to be viewed as the victim offered to the god on the ground of*
> *its hostility to the deity; in short, the god is sacrificed to himself on*
> *the ground that he is his own enemy.*

Frazer's explanation may seem strange at first, but think of God the
Father sacrificing God the Son in Christianity, and the concept at least
comes within the proximity of one's cultural beliefs. If we have difficulty in

accepting the myth of Adonis, Attis, and Osiris, we will also have difficulty in accepting the story of Christ.

The ambiguous attitude toward the pig in mythology is further illustrated in ancient and modern attitudes toward eating pork. The followers of Attis and Adonis did not eat pork, nor did the ancient Egyptians except at certain times. They had two attitudes toward the pig: one as a sacred animal, the other as one to be avoided at all costs. If an Egyptian so much as touched a pig, he would run to the nearest river to bathe. No swineherd was allowed to marry outside his caste, nor to enter any temple. The Hebrews, who inherited many Egyptian ways, placed the pig and the eating of pork on their forbidden list, although some Jews did keep swine.

This taboo of pork is, however, reversed in a unique Estonian tale in which eating pork makes a prince conversant with the language of birds. Most legends, such as that of the Scandinavian Sigurd, make drinking the blood of a dragon accomplish this feat.

In Scandinavian myth the gods and heroes in Valhalla continually feasted upon the magic boar Saehrimir. The number of guests present at the meal varied, depending on how many warriors were killed and picked up by the Valkyries that day, but there was always enough of the animal to go around. The boar was boiled every day and miraculously came alive every morning.

Scandinavian mythology therefore took an entirely different attitude toward the boar and pig from that of the Greeks and Asiatics. The goddess of the Northern Underworld, Freya, had a golden boar made by the dwarfs for her use. She also had a lover Ottar, in the form of a golden boar. Freya's boars were probably symbols of the sun traveling through her Underworld kingdom.

The Christian attitude toward the pig, derived from Hebrew and Egyptian sources, sees the animal as a symbol of sensuality, perhaps unconsciously recalling its connection with fertility goddesses. In Mark's gospel (5:1–20) when Jesus cast out the legion of demons from a madman, the evil spirits fled into a herd of pigs, which then ran down the mountainside and into the sea. When the people learned what had happened, they asked Jesus to leave their country.

Some Bible commentators point out that the people were more worried about the loss of their pigs than about the unfortunate madman. But this is

You are as fat as one of St. Anthony's pigs.

Medieval Proverb

a capitalistic explanation that has no foundation in the legend, which is about the superior strength of one type of spirit over another, weaker one. The tale of the demonic returned to sanity was frequently told in many mythologies of other gods and heroes. Its application to Jesus was a Christian attempt to draw him into an earlier, familiar mythological theme.

In later Christian legend the pig comes in for even more ill-use. The animal is blatantly the devil in the temptation of St. Anthony, a fourth-century monk who spent a good deal of his time fighting off visions of female flesh and of pigs copulating. Anthony's conquest of the devil has supplied Western art with a theme for centuries. Among the best versions of the tale are the grotesque depictions by Bosch and Grünewald, two Northern European minds that reveled in such Gothic horrors. Because Anthony was often pictured with a pig at his feet, the animal had an enviable relationship with his monks, who kept pigs at the public expense. The Christian parishioners supported the beasts so well that it became a proverbial expression of disgust to say one was fat as St. Anthony's pigs.

In the twentieth century the pig has continued to play a large role in popular folklore. Warner Brothers' cartoon creation Porky Pig, the sweet, stuttering, somewhat foolish animal, is beloved by millions of movie fans. Porky is clean, neat, has no genitals, and exemplifies most middle-class American virtues. The irony of Porky Pig is that in many ways he is close to the real thing—the animals are not so dirty as rumor would have us believe. When put in a clean pen, for instance, they keep the pen neat. They are known to be affectionate animals and generally homebodies, although many people persist in using pigs as a symbol of grossness in any form. The head pig in Orwell's *Animal Farm* is a mean, sadistic tyrant employed to exemplify all of man's most horrid traits. The French word for pig, *cochon*, is used to denote disgust or lewdness. Some Americans—Porky Pig notwithstanding—have adopted the custom of shouting "Pigs" at policemen. The character of a pig-policeman in a children's book—although he was a good policeman, doing his duty, not taking bribes—so upset certain police groups as an unfitting image that they asked the publisher to withdraw the book from libraries. But the publisher disagreed and the book continues in circulation.

The pig's paradoxical image in ancient and modern myth—from god to demon; from stuttering, cuddly Porky to sadistic tyrant—sheds much light on man's attitude toward animals in general. In an imaginary dialogue Herodotus portrays Odysseus, Circe, and Gryllus (who had been transformed into a pig by Circe's magic) discussing the merits of being a pig. Gryllus was given the opportunity of returning to human form, but he refused. He found life much more honest as a pig.

ANT AND GRASSHOPPER

One winter's day an ant was drying some grain he had stored in the summer. A grasshopper, dying of hunger, passed by and asked for some food.

"Why didn't you store up some food during the summer?" the ant chastised the grasshopper.

"I didn't have the time," the grasshopper replied. "I spent all the summer singing."

"Well," said the ant, "if you were stupid enough to sing all summer, go and dance all winter!"

This fable from Aesop illustrating the industriousness and diligence of the ant is perhaps the best-known of all that collection. So persistent is the belief in the ant's hardworking character that the Book of Proverbs (6:6) tells the lazy man to follow the ways of the ant and become wise!

The only snag in the folkloric belief is that the ant is not quite so industrious as the tales would have us think. In very cold climates, where the winter is severe, ants go into a semi-dormant state in which they do not eat. In summer their food consists mainly of other insects and sap from trees—things that cannot be stored. If anything, ants display an almost greedy attitude toward food. Honey ants, for instance, constantly feed each other. Some take in enormous amounts of food and their abdomens grow so large that they are forced to cling to the roof of the nest, where they remain in a state of immobility.

The Pueblo Indians of North America might be more aware of the ant's true nature, for they consider the beast to be vindictive and the cause of diseases. In their folklore, illnesses caused by ants can be cured only by an Ant-Doctor. In West Africa an ants' nest is looked upon as the home of demons; while in Hindu mythology ants symbolize the pettiness of all things because of their fragile character and what seems the impotence of their lives.

Yet the Hindus, with their usual dual outlook, also view ant life as superior to human life. The Hindus and Jains feed the ants on certain days, since they believe ants are in some way connected with the dead.

Even more interesting, however, is the belief of the North American Hopi Indians that the first people were ants. This belief is not unrelated to the famous Greek legend of the origin of the Myrmidons, or Ant-Men. Hera, the wife of Zeus, was angry with her husband for being unfaithful to her with a lovely maiden, Aegina. Since the goddess had no means of punishing her husband, nor in this particular instance the girl, she decided to send a plague to ravage the land from which the girl came.

Nothing could stop this plague, and it eventually reduced the population almost to zero. Prayers were in vain. (The suppliants were known to die at the altar with prayers half-said.) There were so many dead that the living fought over wood for the funeral pyres, adding still more casualties.

Finally King Aeacus, the son of Aegina and Zeus, approached the altar of Zeus and begged the god to restore his people to him. There was a clash of thunder, signifying that the god would grant the king's wish. Nearby to Zeus' altar was a sacred oak tree where a troup of ants was busy at work. The king called out to Zeus: "Give me citizens as numerous as these." The tree shook, and there was a rustling in its branches though there was no wind. King Aeacus knew that his prayer would be granted, but how was this repopulation to come about?

That night the king had a dream in which the ants he had seen earlier were turned into men. He awoke from this dream just as his son was telling him to look out the window to see the host of men marching before the palace. The ants had been transformed into warriors.

This new race of men, the Myrmidons, were later noted for their skill as warriors under their leader Achilles during the Trojan War. They did their professional duty so well—following every order scrupulously, regard-less of ethical or moral consideration—that the word is applied to any lackey who follows his leader's word without so much as a tinge of con-science. Who can doubt that today there are millions of Myrmidons—more than could possibly have been descended from the ants seen by the Greek king that day.

ASS AND MULE

Once an ass made friends with a jackal. They broke through the hedge of a cucumber garden and ate what they liked every evening. One night the ass said to the jackal: "What a lovely night. It's perfect for singing."

"My dear friend," replied the jackal, "we don't need any noise now. Thieves and lovers need quiet so they can go about their work. Besides, you don't know how to sing. The watchman will wake up when you open your big mouth."

"What do you know about music?" said the ass. "You live in the forest and are used to rough sounds only. My voice is sweet and lovely."

"That may be true," said the jackal, "but sweet or not, your singing will get us killed by the watchman."

"So you don't think I can sing!" the ass replied angrily.

"Sing if you must," said the jackal. "But wait until I get near the gate."

The ass waited till the jackal reached the gate and then began to bray as loud as he could. The watchman, who had been asleep, came rushing out. He grabbed the ass and beat him, put a halter around his neck, and returned to his nap. The jackal, watching all that happened from a distance, cried to the ass: "Hey, stupid, you had to sing and now you have a necklace for all your effort!"

This Hindu folktale from *The Panchatantra*, a collection of animal fables, presents one of the most common motifs in folklore, the stupidity and hardheadedness of the ass.

Aesop gives us numerous tales in which the ass is shown to be a fool and sometimes, even worse, a vindictive one. In one fable the ass kicks a dying lion, knowing the poor beast cannot strike back. Yet the animal's very stupidity makes him appeal to the more sentimental aspects of man's imagination, whether it be the ass in Lucius Apuleius' Latin novel *The Golden Ass* or the donkey in the Spanish poet Juan Ramón Jiménez' *Platero y Yo,* written in 1914, which recounts the poet's travels with his animal.

The donkey as a means of conveyance is not so comic as it might first appear to an urban person. Asses, not horses, were used by King David and Jesus. The Old Testament counts asses among man's riches along with sheep, cattle, camels, and goats. The Bible even goes so far as to have a talking ass long before Hollywood took up the idea in its series of "Francis the Talking Mule" movies.

The Biblical tale is found in the Book of Numbers (22:4—24:25). The king of Moab tried to bribe Balaam, a Midianite magician, to curse the Israelites as they crossed his land. (Cursing was a very important part of ancient religious practice. Various samples of it can be seen in the Psalms of the Old Testament where the worst calamities are called forth for one's enemies.) Balaam went to Moab, riding on an ass. Suddenly an angel of Yahweh stood invisible before them. The ass, sensing the angel's presence, and not wishing to go through the heavenly messenger, stopped in his tracks. Balaam, who did not see the angel, cursed the animal and finally beat him. The ass turned to the magician and said: "What have I done to thee?"

The angel then revealed himself to Balaam. When the magician reached the court of the king of Moab, he went about his business of cursing the Israelites, but a blessing came out of his mouth instead. The king was furious, but a blessing once uttered could not be recalled.

The Biblical account of the legend does not tell us what happened to the speaking ass. According to later Jewish legend the angel slew the ass to make sure the Jews would not be tempted to worship it as they had earlier the Golden Calf. Yet a Semite belief held that the ass possessed clairvoyance. According to certain Roman writers the ancient Jews worshiped an ass-headed god, and the Jesuits in the seventeenth century accused the Masons of the same crime. One medieval bestiary equates the ass with the devil, since the ass "brays about the place night and day, hour by hour, seeking its prey."

During the Middle Ages, however, the ass was featured in the Feast of Fools, in which the ass on which Jesus made his triumphal entry into Jerusalem was honored. The congregation, upon reaching the end of each prayer, would bray instead of saying "amen."

SCORPION

One day Zeus and Hermes came to visit Hyrieus, a beekeeper. The gods were in disguise and Hyrieus had no idea that he was entertaining divinities. He treated the two so kindly that they revealed themselves to him and said he could have any wish he desired.

"I would like to have a son," the old man replied, "but my wife is long dead and now I am too old. I regret that as a young man I vowed never to have children."

Though Hyrieus was indeed too old, if any god knew myriad ways to father a child it was Zeus. He had changed himself into every shape—animal, mineral, vegetable—to seduce women. Zeus told Hyrieus to sacrifice a bull, urinate on the hide, and bury the hide in his wife's grave. The beekeeper did as the god had instructed, and in nine months Mother Earth brought forth a handsome child who was named Urion ("he who makes water" or urine), which later was corrupted to Orion.

The belief that urine is capable of impregnating is common in much mythology. The famous Greek tale of Danaë and the golden shower, beloved by Renaissance painters, for instance, is actually the mythological expression of Zeus' urinating and thereby fathering a child.

Orion grew up to be a very handsome giant and found himself involved in numerous amours. In one affair he was blinded by the father of his promised wife for raping her before the official nuptials. But his most notorious affair concerned the goddess Artemis. The two got along so well that the goddess was about to marry him. Artemis' brother Apollo, however, was jealous of Orion or wished him for himself, or as one version puts it, Apollo was angry that the young man had slept with Eos the Dawn. (Even today the Dawn blushes for her liaison with the handsome giant.)

Apollo went to Mother Earth and said Orion had boasted he would kill all the beasts of the earth. Mother Earth, of course, could not tolerate this, even though Orion had sprung from her own body. She sent a giant scorpion to attack him. Orion fought as well as he could, but finally gave up and fled into the sea to escape the monster.

"Look!" cried Apollo to Artemis. "That black object in the water! It is Candaon who raped your priestess Opis."

Artemis was taken in by Apollo's lie. She aimed her arrow and shot, hitting Orion through the head. Then, as his body floated by, Artemis realized what she had done. She called Apollo's son Asclepius, the physician, to restore Orion to life. But Zeus struck Apollo's son dead with a thunderbolt, as he would not allow any interference in the life-and-death process. Out of despair the goddess placed Orion in the heavens with the scorpion pursuing him, and to this day he so remains.

In his heavenly position the scorpion rules over one of the signs of the zodiac from October 24 to November 22. Someone born under the sign, according to a seventeenth-century English "Christian horoscope," will be a "pratler without modesty or honesty, a lover of slaughter and quarrels, murder, thievery, a promoter of sedition"; in short, all those things that a seventeenth-century Englishman felt would be most inimical to the maintenance of Jacobean Society.

Though the story of Orion is perhaps the best-known scorpion tale, since he gives his name to the heavenly sign, there is a similar legend among the Egyptians. Set, the evil god, decided to kill Horus, the son of Osiris, god of resurrection. Assuming the form of a scorpion, Set stung and killed Horus. But, in contradiction to the Greek tale, Horus was restored to life by the sun-god Ra.

Gilgamesh, the great hero of the Babylonian epic poem of the same

name, also confronts scorpions. After the death of Enkidu, the great friend
and companion of Gilgamesh, the hero set forth to find the answer to everlasting life. Eventually he came to a mountain named Mashu, which
guarded the rising and the setting of the sun. At the gate of the mountain
scorpions stood guard. They were half men and half animal. Just to look
upon them brought death to the beholder.

When Gilgamesh saw them in the distance he shielded his eyes, but
then his courage made him remove his hand and approach the creatures.
The man-scorpions were quite impressed by Gilgamesh's move. One said to
his companion: "The figure who comes toward us is flesh of the gods."

"Yes," replied his companion, "but only two-thirds is god, the rest is
common man."

They then asked Gilgamesh why he had journeyed so far and what he was
seeking, and he told them.

"When my dear friend Enkidu died, whom I loved more than any mortal
and even the goddess Isthar, I wept for him, hoping he would return to
life. Since then my life is empty without him, so I search for the answer to
life and death."

The man-scorpions told Gilgamesh the journey would be difficult, but
they allowed him to pass the gate of the mountain.

Later Gilgamesh, after his arduous journey, learned that death is the lot
of men, since the gods willed it so.

The rather polite man-scorpions of the *Gilgamesh* epic poem are entirely
missing in Biblical and medieval literature. The scorpion was looked upon
as a demonic being, the poisonous sting at the end of its tail inflicting pain
and death. According to Deuteronomy (8:15) the wilderness was filled
with serpents and scorpions, while in First Kings (12:11) King Rehoboam
threatened his people with a worse yoke than his father, Solomon, had imposed when he said he would chastise them with scorpions.

Jesus in the New Testament (Luke 10:19) gives his disciples authority
and power over scorpions, which symbolized all that opposed his godlike
rule and kingdom. Medieval symbolism chose the animal, therefore, as a
sign of both Judas, the arch-betrayer of Jesus, and the Jews, whom the
medieval Christian saw as opposed to Christ.

Considering the scorpion's generally demonic character, it is interesting to note that medieval folklore recommended placing a dead scorpion on a wound to heal it. Folklore was clever enough, however, to make sure the animal was dead.

GOAT, LAMB, AND RAM

One day the gods Thor and Loki decided to visit the earth. Traveling in Thor's chariot drawn by his two goats, Tooth-gnasher and Gap-tooth, they came to a farmer's house where they decided to stop for the night. During the evening Thor took his goats and slaughtered them for dinner. When the animals were cooked, Thor invited the farmer, his wife, and children to join the feast. They were told they were allowed to eat as much as they liked, provided they did not extract the marrow from the goats' bones. After the meal Thor collected all the bones, put them on the goatskins he had saved, and raised his magic hammer over them, restoring them to life.

Thor then noticed that one of the goats was lame and demanded to know who had eaten the marrow from the goat's leg. The farmer's son admitted he had. Thor was prepared to kill the boy on the spot with his hammer, but the farmer and his wife pleaded with the god to forgive him. The god relented, but on condition that the son and one daughter accompany him on a journey. After a sad parting, the children left with the gods.

The Scandinavian myth does not tell us what happened to the children, but it does indicate clearly that the goat was an early sacrificial animal, a role often found in Greek and Hebrew mythology. For example Hera, the wife of Zeus in Greek mythology, was closely identified with the she-goat at Argos, where youths threw spears at a she-goat during the religious festivals in honor of the goddess. This was supposed to punish the goat for

What was he doing, the great god Pan,
Down in the reeds by the river?
Elizabeth Barrett Browning: *A Musical Instrument*

revealing the hiding place of Hera when once she had fled to the woods to escape her husband's anger.

Usually, however, it was Hera who was angry at Zeus, as when she tried to kill Dionysus, the son of Zeus and Semele. To protect his son Zeus transformed him into a black goat, thereby making the animal sacred to Dionysus as well, who was called "the Kid" or "one of the Black Goatskin." Dionysus' followers would tear to pieces a live goat and devour its raw flesh (a custom still practiced in present-day Algeria by a mystical sect unrelated to Dionysus). Euripides, in his brilliant play *The Bacchants*, captures the joy and ecstasy of those who followed Dionysus:

> . . . *the rhythmic beat of the drums;*
> *The squeal of the flutes . . . Look, He*
> *Comes, Dionysus, from the wild packs,*
> *Wearing a holy-faun skin. He hunts*
> *The wild goat, killing it and tearing*
> *Its raw flesh for food . . . !"*

Dionysus replaced an earlier goat-god figure who protected the vines from blight. Dionysus' role as wine-god (better known by the Latin form of his name, Bacchus) inspired one of the early statues by Michelangelo, showing a handsome youth, somewhat drunk, holding a cup in his hand— with a small, childlike satyr near his legs. Dionysus, however, was not alone in his goatlike nature in Greek mythology. Pan, Silenus, satyrs, and fauns also shared the goat's nature in part, making the goat an ideal symbol of the excessive sexuality which these gods and creatures were believed to possess. When one calls a man an "old goat," it still refers to this lecherous nature. Folktales have many references to the sexual practices of goats. One tale tells of a husband who transformed himself into a goat so as to watch his wife's adultery.

Goats abound in Greek mythological families, for aside from Hera's and Dionysus' identification with the beast, Zeus was nursed by a goat, Amaltheia, when he was hidden from his devouring father Cronus as a child. Later, after Zeus had defeated his father, one of Amaltheia's horns broke off and Zeus turned it into the Cornucopia, or the Horn of Plenty. A variation of the Greek legend says Amaltheia was a nymph who nursed Zeus with the milk of a goat. Later she was placed in the heavens in the sign of Capricorn. The goat-fish, connected with the Capricorn sign, was created when Pan and other Greek divinities fled the demon Typhon. Pan leaped into the Nile before he had completely taken on the goat form he had chosen, thus becoming half-goat and half-fish.

Pan's mixed animal nature was better than that of his Hebrew counterpart, Azazel, "goat of removal' or "God strengthens," who was a wild demon of the desert, perhaps descended from an earlier goat-god. On the Day of Atonement a priest would cast lots between two goats. The one that fell to Yahweh was sacrificed, while the one that fell to Azazel was led into the desert as the scapegoat, carrying the sins of the people. (Leviticus 16:7–10.)

In Matthew's gospel (25:32–34) Jesus says he will separate the sheep from the goats, signifying the goats as the souls of the damned. Yet a medieval bestiary says Christ is like a goat, since his eyes are as sharp as a goat's and can see everything. The lamb symbol, however, has been applied from earliest times to Christ, to many saints, and to the individual Christian. The

Biblical references to Jesus as the Lamb of God are numerous. When John the Baptist saw Jesus in the distance, he called out to his followers: "Behold the Lamb of God, which taketh away the sin of the world" (John 1:29). The verse recalls the fact that lambs were sacrificed to commemorate the Exodus from Egypt. Some Christian commentators on the verse explain that as the Exodus freed man from physical bondage, so Christ frees man from the bondage of the devil.

The ram, a male sheep, is found as a symbol of numerous gods such as Ammon-Ra, Osiris, Qeb, and Shu in Egyptian mythology. The ram was sacrificed to Ammon-Ra once each year. It was skinned and the skin placed over an image of the god, recalling the time when Ammon-Ra was incarnated in the form of a ram. In Hinduism the ram is the steed of the fire-god Agni. The ram is also one of the ten animals admitted to the Moslem heaven because of its connection with Abraham.

In Genesis (22:13) Yahweh provided a ram for Abraham to sacrifice in place of his son Isaac. According to Jewish folklore the ram had been caught in the thicket from the sixth day of Creation and was waiting for Abraham and Isaac to come along. From the bones of the sacred ram the foundations of the Holy of Holies was built; its veins became the strings of King David's harp; its skin was made into the belt and girdle of Elijah; its left horn made the shofar used by Moses on Mount Sinai; and its right horn the shofar which the Prophet Elijah will blow on Mount Moriah to announce the coming of the Messiah.

RABBIT

Once upon a time there was a great drought. All the streams and creeks went dry in the forest. The animals met to see what they could do. The lion, the bear, the wolf, the fox, and even the rabbit, came to the meeting. They decided to dig a well. Everybody would pitch in to help, but the rabbit said he didn't want to work.

"If you don't dig the well," said the lion, "you don't drink its water."

The rabbit just laughed at the lion. "You dig the well," said the rabbit. "I'll get the water."

So all the animals worked away at digging the well. Then they drank their fill and went to their homes to sleep. The next morning they saw the rabbit's footprints near the well and knew he had stolen some water. They decided to set up a guard at the well.

The bear was chosen to watch, and he took up his post when night fell. In a short time the rabbit came out of a thicket and saw the bear at the well. At first the rabbit was at a loss for what to do, but then he decided on a plan. He began to sing very sweetly! The bear, hearing the sweet music, got up and looked around.

"Where's all that pretty music coming from?" he said.

The rabbit sang on and the bear, carried away by the music started to dance. He danced and danced until he was quite away from the well. Then the rabbit, no longer fearful of the bear, went and drank from the well.

The next day the animals were mad at the bear for being such a fool. Although they could see the rabbit's footprints near the well, the bear insisted the rabbit hadn't come. Then the animals placed a monkey to guard the well at night, but the same thing happened again. Finally the fox said: "I know what we should do. Let's make a tar baby and set him to watch the well tonight." All the animals agreed. They set about making a handsome tar baby, which they placed at the well, and then went home for their night's rest.

The rabbit came along, saw the tar baby, and began to sing again. The tar baby didn't move. The rabbit kept on singing, but the tar baby didn't seem to hear anything at all. Finally the rabbit came close, but the tar baby didn't speak.

"Look here," said the rabbit, "you get out of my way or I'll knock you down!" The tar baby didn't answer, and the rabbit grew even madder. "Get out of my way or I'll hit you with my fist!" the rabbit screamed out.

No answer. So the rabbit hit the tar baby, but his fist stuck in the tar. Then he kicked the tar baby, but his feet stuck and he couldn't move at all. Next morning all the animals came and saw that their scheme had worked— the rabbit was caught.

"You won't steal any more water from us," said the lion. "Now we're going to cut off your head."

"That's just the way I want to die," said the rabbit.

"Well," replied the lion, "we certainly won't kill you the way you want."

"Let's shoot him!" cried the bear.

"Oh, that's an even better way to die," cooed the rabbit.

"I know what to do," said the bear. "Let's make him fat with food. Then when he's as big as can be, we'll toss him up in the air and let him burst when he hits the ground."

"No, no!" cried the rabbit. "Don't stuff me and burst me." So the animals put the rabbit in a cupboard and fed him sweets and cakes every day until he was quite fat. Then they took him out on the hillside. The lion took the rabbit's paw, held him up, and began to swing him back and forth. At last he tossed the rabbit into the air. The rabbit came down on his feet with a thump, and crying:

"Yip, my name's Molly cotton-tail,
Catch me if you can."

The Tar Baby tale, as it is usually designated, is a very ancient folktale known in numerous African and American versions. It was probably brought to North America by the first African slaves and transformed to an American setting as time went on. The tale given above is based on one version from West Virginia, though the version given by Joel Chandler Harris in his *Uncle Remus, His Songs and Sayings* is perhaps better known. Chandler's book inspired the popular Disney motion picture *Song of the South*, which combined live actors and animated cartoon characters. Its popularity made the antics of Br'er Rabbit known to a much wider audience than had been possible through folktales and books.

Br'er Rabbit's cleverness and deception reflect the joy people have in seeing a smaller and weaker animal or person victorious over the stronger and larger force. Perhaps the captive Africans could identify with Br'er Rabbit as he outwitted the bear and the wolf.

Another tale from South Carolina points up amusingly the cleverness of Br'er Rabbit over Br'er Wolf, who probably represented the slave owner.

There was a big dance and Br'er Rabbit and Br'er Wolf were invited. Both animals, however, wanted to take the same girl to the dance. The rabbit told the girl that the wolf could not go, since Br'er Wolf served as Br'er Rabbit's riding horse. When the wolf heard about this, he became very angry and demanded Br'er Rabbit tell the girl the truth.

"I'm too sick to travel," answered Br'er Rabbit.

"I'll carry you halfway," said Br'er Wolf, "but you've got to tell her that I'm not your riding horse."

"I can't ride unless I have a saddle," replied Br'er Rabbit.

So Br'er Wolf put on a saddle and Br'er Rabbit mounted it. The rabbit, unknown to the wolf, also put on spurs. When they had gone halfway, Br'er Wolf told Br'er Rabbit to get off, but the rabbit locked his spurs into the poor wolf, making him run all the way to the girl's house.

"See," said Br'er Rabbit, "I told you Br'er Wolf was my riding horse!"

While in most modern literature the rabbit is sentimentalized, as in the *Peter Rabbit* tales, animated cartoons still capture the clever, trickster nature of the rabbit, as in the well-known Warner Brothers creation of Bugs Bunny. This clever bunny is cruel (he admits it) and smart. He outwits those larger and supposedly cleverer than he, such as Elmer Fudd, the sad human whom he continually tortures and gets into difficulties. Bugs is actually quite a demonic character, and it is not suprising that he is one of the most popular cartoon characters ever created.

Bugs Bunny's trickster nature is shared by a host of other rabbits in world mythology, extending back to the Hindu *The Panchatantra.* Yet alongside this devilish, trickster nature the life-giving beneficent role of the rabbit is also prominent. The Algonquin Indians of North America, for instance, believed the great hare, Manabozho or Manabush, was the incarnation of all life-giving energy. He was the creator, provider of food and medicine men to the Algonquins. One of his most famous exploits was the destruction of the great fish, who in this myth was a symbol of evil. Manabozho let the evil fish swallow him, then cut his way out, thereby killing the demon. Like Prometheus, Manabozho also stole fire from heaven and gave it to man. The Algonquins believed the great hare lived in the Far West in the village of souls.

Buddhist legend tells of a hare that sacrificed its life to appease Buddha's hunger. As a reward it was sent to the moon, where it now sits, making the elixir of life. The man in the moon then is a hare, according to Buddhist myth, as he is in Aztec mythology, where it was once believed that the moon was as bright as the sun until the latter darkened the moon by casting a hare into its face.

From the amusing antics of the rabbit it is difficult to understand why it came to be considered a melancholy animal by the ancient Greeks and the medieval Europeans. Rabbit flesh was supposed to bring melancholia to those who ate it. Shakespeare's Falstaff tells Prince Hal that he is as melancholy as a hare, while Lady Answerwell in Swift's *Polite Conversation* will not eat rabbits because " 'Tis a melancholy meat."

This reputation did not, however, stop people from eating rabbit meat in the hope of promoting fertility, since the animal, sacred to the goddess Aphrodite, was a symbol of fecundity. Pliny says that eating rabbit would remove barrenness, and his advice was still being followed well into the

Renaissance, where concoctions of pulverized rabbit flesh were eaten to insure fertility.

During the Middle Ages wedding rings often depicted a rabbit to insure the couple would produce enough children, though Christian symbolists considered the rabbit a sign of lust. When a white hare was shown next to the Virgin Mary in many medieval and Renaissance paintings, for instance, it indicated the triumph of Chastity over Lust, symbolized respectively by the Virgin and Hare.

According to American Indian Huron mythology, however, Ioskeha or Iouskeha, the white rabbit, created both animals and mankind after he drove off his evil twin brother, Tawiscara, or the Dark One. In Potawatomi American Indian legend, Messou, who corresponds to Ioskeha, restored the earth after a great flood had destroyed it. Although he is a creator, the rabbit is also a trickster.

Does the image seem to fit the white rabbit in Lewis Carroll's *Alice's Adventures in Wonderland*? One wonders if the retiring clergyman had a volume of American Indian mythology safely tucked away in his library.

RAT AND MOUSE

Hatto, a tenth-century German prelate, was noted in his early life for his holiness and the efficient way in which he ruled his monastery. In reward for his services to the Church he was appointed Bishop of Mainz. Some time after his installation a famine devastated the countryside and the neighboring people came to the good bishop for help, knowing he had amassed vast stores of wheat in his granaries. The bishop, although annoyed by their request (apparently his new position had corrupted his soul), nevertheless appointed a day for the people to receive the grain. When the day arrived, the crowd filled the bishop's barn to capacity. The bishop then locked the door and set the barn on fire, burning all the people to death.

The destruction of his flock did not seem to have any adverse effect on Hatto, who proceeded to his dinner and a good night's sleep. Next morning he saw that his portrait had been eaten by rats. As the bishop was mulling the destroyed piece of vanity, a servant rushed in to tell him rats had also eaten all the stored wheat. No sooner had the servant told his tale when another appeared to inform the bishop that the rats were en route to the palace. Hatto, looking out the window, could see thousands of the creatures descending upon the building.

In terror he fled by boat to a private island where he had earlier built a tower. His flight, however, was in vain; the rats pursued him, attacked his boat, and landed on the island. The bishop managed to reach the tower,

They have whetted their teeth against the stones,
And now they pick the Bishop's bones;
They gnaw'd the flesh from every limb,
For they were sent to do judgement on him.

Robert Southey: *Metrical Tales.*

but the rats caught up with him and ate him alive.

This grisly tale from medieval Germany is repeated in many European folk traditions. Numerous "mouse towers" exist with similar tales attached to them, indicating a time perhaps when people were sacrificed to a rat-god. In a Polish version it is a king and his family who are destroyed by mice after the king liquidated all the nobles who had opposed him. Avenging mice issued from the bodies of the slain men, reflecting a belief that mice were the souls of the dead.

Another German tale illustrates this latter belief. A servant girl fell asleep while shelling nuts. Her companions observed a red mouse creep out of her mouth and run to the nearby window. One of the men present shook the girl but could not wake her. He then moved her to another spot. When the mouse ran back, it dashed about looking for the girl. Not finding her, it vanished—and at the same moment the girl died.

The rat's connection with the soul and death is a prevalent theme in most European mythologies and has been passed on to Christianity. The pagan Germans, for instance, worshiped a goddess called Nehalennia or Hludana, whose symbol was the rat and whose function was to accompany the souls of the dead. In medieval European symbolism the goddess was turned into the twelfth-century St. Gertrude, who was invoked by the living for the souls of the dead. The saint was nearly always pictured with a rat as her companion. One Christian explanation for the symbol is that Gertrude was so absorbed in prayer she did not notice rats running up and down her pastoral staff; another version says the rat, being a symbol of evil, was overcome by Gertrude.

Saints and pagan goddesses were not the only ones associated with rats and mice. Sinners also found the creatures useful. Witches were said to make mice out of pears through the proper incantations. However, their mice lacked tails, because only God could create a perfect creature, while at best witches could only caricature God's world.

The mouse was one symbol of the Greek god Apollo in his role as sender of plague, and as the sun-god who dispelled the forces of night symbolized by mice and rats. Apollo was appealed to as *"O Smintheus,"* or "O Mouse," when he was invoked in his role as sender of plague. Many ancient peoples realized that there was some connection between mice and plague, though the scientific explanation was unknown to them. The rat is often a symbol of night, since it frees the lion, the symbol of the sun, in so many tales. The well-known Aesop fable tells of a mouse that was one day spared by a lion. In return, when the mouse later saw the lion caught in a net, he gnawed away at it and the lion was freed.

The prevalence of the rat as a night symbol is found illustrated in a tale of E. T. A. Hoffmann which was used as the basis for Tchaikovsky's *Nutcracker* ballet. The Mouse-King in the tale had seven gold crowns, like the dragon in the Book of Revelation (12:3). When the Mouse-King was defeated by the Nutcracker, who then turned into a handsome prince, there was a sudden burst of brilliant light upon the heroine, who found herself in the midst of a fragrant meadow that glittered as if strewn with precious stones.

The mouse's generally demonic role in mythology is offset in Pop culture by the character of Mickey Mouse. Walt Disney's cartoon character first appeared in *Steamboat Willie* in 1928, humming and singing his way to a fortune—and continuing to this day, the mouse perhaps being no longer a symbol of night, but of a successful business enterprise.

SPIDER

Once there was a beautiful maiden named Arachne, who was so accomplished in the arts of spinning and weaving that the nymphs would leave their groves and fountains just to come and gaze upon her at work. Her work was not only beautiful when it was done, but her manner of work was a thing of beauty in itself. To watch her one would have said the goddess Athene herself, who had invented spinning, had been Arachne's teacher. But Arachne was heard to scorn the idea that a goddess had taught her the art.

"Let Athene try her skill with mine," she boasted. "If beaten, I will pay the penalty."

Athene heard this and, assuming the form of an old woman, appeared to Arachne. She kindly advised her to challenge her fellow mortals, but to ask forgiveness of the goddess. Arachne told the old woman to mind her own business.

"I'm not afraid of the goddess," she said. "Let her try her skill if she has the courage."

At that moment the old woman's form changed into that of the goddess, and all those near fell and worshiped her. All, that is, except Arachne, who was unmoved.

The contest began. Athene wrought on her loom the scene of her contest with the sea-god Poseidon. All the twelve Olympian gods were pictured with Zeus in the midst of the work. But what was most arresting about her work was that the goddess purposefully worked in incidents at the corners, illustrating the displeasure of the gods at presumptuous mortals.

Arachne again, in spite of this second warning, was unmoved. She filled her loom with sexual scenes of the gods and goddesses. Athene was impressed but, being a goddess, vengeful as well. She struck the web with her shuttle and broke it into pieces. Then she beat Arachne until the young maiden, finally brought down, hanged herself.

"Live, guilty woman," declared Athene, "but so you always remember this lesson, continue to hang forever—both you and all your descendants."

Sprinkling Arachne with the juices of aconite, the goddess transformed her into a spider, spinning the thread by which she was suspended.

This tale from Ovid's *Metamorphoses* shows the goddess giving Arachne at least two warnings before meting out the punishment. In another version of the legend Athene easily surpasses the workmanship of Arachne and nevertheless transforms the maiden into a spider as a warning to other mortals who would presume upon the gods. Dante uses Arachne's tale of presumption as an example of pride in the Purgatory of *The Divine Comedy*. Robert Graves in his book *The Greek Myths* suggests, in a less moralistic vein, that the tale might record the early commercial rivalry between the Athenians and the Lydio-Carian sea rulers, who were of Cretan origin. The mother city Carian Miletus was a large exporter of dyed woolens and seriously rivaled Athens, the city of the goddess.

Other folklores see the spider not as the victim of the gods but as an agent of the deities. The Chibcha Indians, a North Andean tribe, believe for example that the dead cross the lake of death on boats made of spider webs. They therefore hold the spider in awe and will not kill it. Some South American Indian mythologies believed the spider web to be the means of climbing from the "lower world" to the "upper world," much as Jacob's ladder symbolized the communion between gods and men in Genesis. In an African myth Yiyi, a Spider-man, brings fire from heaven to help mankind, as Prometheus does in Greek mythology. Yiyi's web is used by the handmaidens of the sun to come down to earth to draw water and then reascend to heaven.

Belief in the beneficent aspects of the spider finds support in many

"Will you walk into my parlour?" said a Spider to a Fly;
"'Tis the prettiest little parlour that ever you did spy."

Mary Howitt: *The Spider and The Fly*

legends. When Mohammed fled from his enemies at Mecca, he hid in a cave. Suddenly in front of the cave a tree grew, then a wood pigeon nested in it, and finally a spider wove a web between the tree and the cave. When the Koreishites, the Prophet's enemies, saw the web they concluded no one had entered the cave recently, and so the Prophet was left unharmed. There is a similar legend told about Jesus when hiding from Herod's cruelty.

History, blended with legend, supplies two more instances of the helpfulness of a spider. Perhaps the best-known one in the English-speaking world concerns Robert the Bruce, the fourteenth-century Scottish hero-king. While hiding from the English on the island of Rathlin, he watched a spider trying to weave its web across a portion of the ceiling. The spider tried six times to reach the far side but failed each time. As he saw the spider begin its seventh try, Robert is reported to have said: "Now shall this spider teach me what I am to do, for I also have failed six times." The spider succeeded on that seventh try, as Robert later did in his seventh try against the English armies.

The spider may have taught Robert the Bruce a lesson, but according to a guidebook it actually saved the life of Frederick the Great. That monarch was about to drink a cup of chocolate in a room of his castle Sans Souci when he set the cup down to reach for a handkerchief. Then he turned back and found a large spider had fallen into the drink. Naturally he asked for another cup of chocolate. The cook, thinking his plot to poison the monarch had been discovered, shot himself. Frederick was thankful to the spider, and tradition has it that he had painted upon the room's ceiling a large spider.

After all this good report on the spider we have now to deal with the less savory aspects of its reputation. In European legend it is considered a loathsome animal who traps the unwary fly. As one English bestiary of the Middle Ages puts it, with careful emphasis on the female sex of the spider:

> *She comes anon to the net,*
> *Takes the fly in the trap she set. . . .*

This couplet, from a much longer poem, was echoed centuries later in Hollywood cartoons of the 1930s. The spider is shown as a vile, loathsome creature akin to a vampire, luring defenseless insects to their doom. In one animated cartoon the spider is undone through the concerted efforts of the flies, who organize an effective fighting force, perhaps displaying a bit of contemporary social commentary on the part of the film's makers.

It would be unfair to the spider's mythological reputation, however, to leave it on such a demonic note. According to the mythology of Nauru Island in the South Pacific the world was created by Areop-Enap, or Ancient Spider.

At first there was only Areop-Enap floating in endless space. One day he found a mussel, opened it after great effort, and crawled inside. It was so dark that Areop-Enap had to move about very carefully. Then he found in the darkness a snail and from it made the moon, but having no place to hang it, he formed the sky from a worm. Finally another snail was made into the sun, and then the mussel shell split to form the earth. From the salt sweat of Areop-Enap's body he formed the primordial sea, and as a final act he turned stones into men, who held up the sky.

ELEPHANT

To avoid being annoyed by her husband Siva while she was bathing, the Hindu goddess Parvati created a servant from the sweat of her body and the dust of the ground. Her servant-guardian, Ganesha, or Chief-of-Troops, watched the door of her bath against the intrusion of Siva, who apparently liked to make love to his wife in the bath. Siva, not one to be put off by any guard at his wife's door, tried to make his way past Ganesha by calling in a troop of demons to do away with this obstruction, but Ganesha fought them off. To aid the demons the gods also entered the fray but to no avail, for Ganesha held demons and gods at bay.

Finally the god Vishnu thought of a way to divert Ganesha's attention. Suddenly he made a beautiful maiden appear, who so excited Ganesha that he turned to watch her, and one of Vishnu's men cut off Ganesha's head.

Parvati was furious that one of her creations should be so treated. She went on a rampage among the gods that was even worse than their battle with Ganesha. She demanded that Ganesha be restored to life—head and all. To appease the goddess, Siva sent the gods on a mission, asking them to bring back the head of the first animal they came upon. It was an elephant, and from that day Ganesha has been Gajanana, or Elephant-face.

In another version Ganesha was still in his cradle when the gods and demi-gods came to visit him, all except Shani, or Saturn. When his mother Parvati noticed this breech of eiquette, she complained as to why the god had not come to show his respects to her baby. After all, Parvati wanted to show off the child. Parvati was told Shani had not come because he feared harm to the child. It was known that anyone Shani looked upon turned to ashes.

"Not *my* baby!" cried the goddess.

She had Shani come to pay his respects to mother and child. When Shani looked at the baby Ganesha, the child's head instantly disappeared in burst of flame.

The goddess demanded that the head of her child be restored, but Shani pointed to the ashes on the floor, saying it was now impossible.

"Then send forth a servant and let him bring me the head of the first one he meets," the goddess cried out. And so it was a poor elephant that lost his head as a result.

The elephant-headed Ganesha is one of the most popular gods in the Hindu pantheon. Nearly every Indian home has a shrine to him to bring good luck. No venture is started without prayers first to Ganesha to ask his protection for the undertaking. Ganesha is usually pictured with a corpulent human body and four hands. He rides a rat as his mount and has a snake for a belt. And he is missing one tusk.

The loss of one tusk has two Hindu myths to account for it. In one, the god was listening to the author of *The Mahabharata* and was so touched that he removed his tusk to write down some of the verses. In the other myth the god threw his tusk at the moon when it laughed at him for eating so many sweet cakes. When Ganesha's tusk hit it, the moon blacked out and the people prayed to the gods to restore the light of evening. Ganesha was begged (he can never be forced) to restore the moon's light. The god answered the prayer in part; that is why the moon waxes and wanes, whereas before it was always bright.

Ganesha's mount, the rat, is the symbol of a powerful demon the god overcame, for Ganesha is a symbol of spiritual strength and the rat is of lower nature in Hinduism. The god also wears a serpent belt. When Ganesha, riding his rat, tripped over a serpent, his belly split open and hundreds upon hundreds of sweet cakes rolled out. The god angrily grabbed the snake and made a belt to hold in his stomach after he had refilled it with the sweet cakes.

Praise to thee, O Ganesa. Thou art manifestly the
truth . . . the Supreme Brahma, the eternal Spirit. . . .

Ganapati Upanishad

India has numerous elephant tales and legends in addition to those of Ganesha. They are both Hindu and Buddhist, since the animal figured prominently in Indian life. Elephants were used in warfare, as a citadel from which the leaders watched the battle, and could be possessed only by members of royalty.

Even more important to India was the elephant's role as bringer of rain. White elephants in particular were important because they could attract their celestial relatives, the clouds, which are heavenly rain-bearing elephants. If a ruler did away with a white elephant, his people would feel betrayed. In one *Tale of the Former Existences of the Buddha,* the Buddha gave away the white elephant of his father to a nearby country suffering from drought and famine. The king's subjects felt betrayed and forced the Buddha into exile.

Buddha's birth was also connected with an elephant. His mother Queen Maya of Nepal had a dream that a white elephant with six tusks, who lived in the Golden Mountain, had entered her body. When she told her dream to the soothsayers, they said she would either bear a son who would rule the world or one who would save it. She bore the latter, the Buddha.

Perhaps one of the most touching Hindu tales of the high respect the elephant enjoyed concerns a sage named Gautama, not to be confused with the Buddha. He found a baby elephant that had lost its mother and was very sad. The good man took the elephant and nursed him until he was big and strong. One day Indra, the great sky-god, looked down from heaven at the large elephant, which he wanted for himself. So taking the form of a king, he went to the sage and offered gold and servants in exchange for the young elephant.

"Don't take my elephant," cried the sage. "He brings me fuel and water, guards my hermitage when I am away, and is gentle and obedient. I love him dearly."

But the god insisted he would take the elephant, since only kings had the right to such majestic beasts. Gautama said he would follow the king no matter where he went—to hell or heaven. Then suddenly Gautama realized he was speaking to a god. He apologized but still would not say the god could take his elephant. Indra was so pleased with Gautama that he took the sage and the elephant to heaven with him, thus gaining the advice of the sage as well as the possession of the elephant.

Julius Caesar had no such romantic notions about elephants. He thought the animal fit only for a circus show. When he sent his well-known *"Veni, vidi, vinci"* message, he also sent along to Rome forty elephants. When Caesar returned from Gaul, he paraded in triumph between these twenty pairs of elephants. Caesar had no interest, however, in the animal's possibilities in war.

On the other hand Plutarch, in his short treatise on animals, credits the elephant with being kind, loving, faithful, and intelligent. He tells a tale of an elephant who was being trained in a difficult balancing act. The creature was having some difficulty keeping up with his elephant brothers. At night, however, the elephant was seen practicing in the moonlight all by himself.

The reference to moonlight betrays the ancient belief that at the waxing of the moon, elephants would gather long branches from forest trees and raise them rhythmically in their trunks as homage to the Queen of the Night. This rather fanciful suggestion makes an exciting picture. There was an even stranger ancient notion that the animal had no joints in its legs. This idea is quite inexplicable, since many of the ancients did see real elephants. According to the belief an elephant could not bend its knees. Once fallen down, it had to stay that way! How then did the elephant rest when it was tired? One answer is given by Isidore of Seville, a seventh-century saint who appears to have made a lifework of collecting as much misinformation as possible for his encyclopedia.

The saint says the tired elephant cannot lie down but must lean against a strong tree. If the tree breaks, the elephant will never be able to get up. This widespread belief continued well into the seventeenth century.

Although these unscientific beliefs on elephant behavior no longer have any validity, the elephant's reputation as a good, lovable animal is still with us in such characters as Dumbo the elephant and sweet Babar—two fictional creations that as part of today's Pop culture are fascinating youngsters who have not read Plutarch or Isidore of Seville.

My soul is as a sacred bird....
Hafiz: *Ode XIV*

PART THREE
Animals of the Air

BIRDS

Many years ago there was a very holy man, one of the monks in a monastery. He was kneeling one day at his prayers in the garden of his monastery when he heard a little bird singing in one of the rosebushes. Never had he heard anything in the world so sweet as the song of that little bird.

And the little bird, after singing for some time longer, flew away to a distant grove. The holy man followed the bird, for he felt he would never tire listening to that sweet song. The little bird went away to another distant tree, sang there for a while, then to another, and so on. The holy man still followed it, farther and farther from the monastery, ever delighting in its enchanting song.

But at last he was obliged to give up, as it was growing late in the day, and he returned to the monastery. As he approached, the sun was setting with all the most heavenly colors ever seen, and when he came into the monastery, it was nightfall.

He was quite surprised at everything he saw, for all the faces about him were strange, the very place itself appearing to have been altered. Nothing seemed as it was when he had left in the morning, not even the garden where he had been kneeling at his devotion when he first heard the singing of the little bird.

While he was wondering at all he saw, one of the monks came up to him.

So the holy man questioned him: "Brother, what is the cause of all these strange changes that have taken place here since the morning?"

The monk, greatly puzzled at his question, asked him what he meant by the changes since morning. Surely there had been no change; all was just as before. And then the monk said: "Brother, why do you ask these strange questions, and what is your name? For you wear the habit of our order, though we have never seen you before."

At this the holy man told his name. He also stated that he had wandered away from the garden, listening to the song of a little bird that was singing in one of the rosebushes near where he was kneeling at his prayers.

The brother gazed earnestly at the holy man as he spoke, then told him of a tradition in the monastery that a brother of his name had left it two hundred years before, never to be heard from again.

While he was speaking the holy man said: "My hour of death is come; blessed be the name of the Lord for all his mercies to me, through the merits of his only begotten Son."

Although this Irish folktale ends with the Christian explanation that the "little bird was an angel" come to take the holy man to God, it does contain the earlier mythological motif of the bird as a messenger of death.

In Welsh folklore there is Aderyne y Corph, a supernatural bird that foretells the death of a person. According to English folklore the cry of a whippoorwill near a house indicates the coming death of one of its inhabitants, while a bird tapping at a window or flying into a house signifies that someone who lives in the house will meet death within a year.

The bird was chosen as the messenger of death since in many mythologies it is believed to be the spirit of some dead soul. It is thus one spirit calling another to join it in the other world.

This belief is found in Egypt where the Ba, or soul, is depicted as a hawk with a human head. The Ba abandoned the body at death and hovered over the mummy until it reentered the body to protect it from decay. After the body was placed in its tomb, the Ba flew about the area of burial at night. The Egyptians left cakes to feed the Ba to insure that the spirit would not come and harm them.

One Hindu tale tells of an ogre who was questioned by his daughter about the location of his soul. The ogre replied, "Sixteen miles away from this place is a tree. Round the tree are tigers and bears and scorpions and snakes; on the top of the tree is a very great fat snake; on his head is a little cage, in the cage is a bird; and my soul is in that bird."

In Jewish folklore the bird Hoyl was the only creature that refused to eat the forbidden fruit when Adam gave it to all the animals after he and Eve had eaten of it. The Hoyl, therefore, does not know death but like the Phoenix goes to sleep, a divine fire consuming it and its nest. All that remains is an egg, which miraculously hatches a new, full-grown Hoyl.

One of the most interesting Jewish legends concerns the seduction of Bathsheba by King David. According to the legend, one day while David was writing a psalm the devil came into the room in the form of a glorious bird. Its feathers were pure gold, its beak made of diamonds, its legs of rubies. David, who loved the physical aspects of life as much as the spiritual, tried to snare the bird, which he believed came from the Garden of Eden. The bird flew out of the window and settled on the branch of a tree in a nearby garden. And who should be under that tree but a young woman named Bathsheba.

King Solomon, the offspring of David's and Bathsheba's lust, was noted in Jewish folklore for his converse with the birds as well as for his great wisdom.

One day Solomon commanded all the birds to appear before him at court. They all came except for the cockerel, who was later asked to explain his absence. The bird told Solomon he had been flying all over the world and saw a beautiful city ruled by a woman. She was the Queen of Sheba, whose city worshiped idols. The bird then suggested to the king that a band of birds descend on the city to destroy it. Solomon did not take this advice. (The idea of birds as destructive was centuries later used by Alfred Hitchcock to chilling effect in his movie *The Birds.*) Hearing how lovely the Queen of Sheba was, Solomon decided that she should visit him. This message was related via a bird, and the great queen came to the king.

King Solomon was not alone in the gift of understanding the language of birds. One of the most persistent motifs regarding birds in nearly all mythology and folklore is their ability to speak and be understood by humans. All a person has to do is learn to understand birds and a whole new world is opened to him or to her. St. Rose of Lima, a sixteenth-century saint, sang verses to the birds during her mystical transports, and according to legend the birds answered her and she understood them. The saint's gift was given to her by God, though sometimes in mythology and folklore the gift is acquired through other means. Sigurd, the great Northern hero, tasted dragon's blood and subsequently could understand the language of birds. In one Grimm fairy tale, *The White Snake,* a servant ate part of a king's supper and as a result could understand the language of birds and other animals.

What do the birds say? In folklore they often give a warning (as they do to Sigurd) or a prophecy, or some sign of love. According to Konrad Lorenz in *King Solomon's Ring* birds can fall in love with humans, completely disdaining their own kindred. Lorenz writes that birds reared in isolation tend "to regard human beings, and human beings only, as potential partners in all reproductive activities." Certainly Lorenz does not sound too out of joint, since the Roman poet Catullus tells how some Roman women used birds for sexual intercourse. What Catullus does not tell us is what the birds said to the women.

EAGLE, HAWK, AND VULTURE

One day an eagle met a serpent and started a conversation with him.

"Why don't we swear an oath of friendship and peace?" suggested the eagle. "If one of us breaks the oath, may Shamash, god of justice, punish the offender."

The serpent agreed and swore an oath with the eagle, promising to help him hunt food—and the eagle promised to help the serpent also. The serpent caught goats and kids for the eagle, while the eagle killed wild bulls and asses for the serpent. The arrangement worked well, for both eagle and serpent prospered, each having numerous offspring. When the eagle's young ones had grown up, he decided it was time to do away with the serpent and his brood. One eaglet, however, warned his father that it was evil to go against an oath to the god Shamash. But the father, paying no attention to his wise son, killed the young serpents.

When the old serpent saw what had happened, he cried out to Shamash for justice: "I put all my trust in you, Shamash. The eagle has destroyed my young and torn my nest apart!"

The god, hearing the plea, told the serpent to pass over to the other side of the mountain, where he would find the carcass of a wild bull. The serpent was then to hide inside the bull and wait for the eagle to swoop down.

"When the eagle enters the carcass, tear off his wings, strip him of feathers, and cast him into a pit so he will die of hunger and thirst," the god said.

The serpent hid as Shamash had commanded, and the eagle, again against the wise advice of his son, descended upon the bull's carcass and the snake attacked him.

Left in a pit to die, the eagle prayed every day to Shamash to forgive and save him. The god, having pity on the eagle, said he would give him life on condition that he help one man, Etana. The man had prayed daily to the great god for the Plant of Life so he could have a son, for his marriage was childless, a great disgrace in the ancient world.

Etana, guided by Shamash, came upon the eagle as he was praying and promised to save him. Etana lifted the eagle from the pit and gave him food. After regaining his strength, the eagle said to Etana: "We are friends now. Tell me what you want and I'll do it."

"I want the Plant of Life," Etana replied, "so I can have a son."

The man then mounted the eagle's back and ascended with him to the various heavens. As they rose higher and higher Etana became fearful, but the eagle continued his flight. At last it was too much for the man. He became dizzy, fell down to earth, and died.

The first part of this Sumerian myth presents the age-old conflict between the eagle and the serpent. In Greek mythology the eagle, for example, was sacred to Zeus, while the serpent was sacred to Hera, Zeus' wife and the earth-goddess. The eagle served Zeus in his adventures to satisfy his lust. When Zeus fell madly in love with a Trojan boy Ganymede, he took the form of an eagle, swooped down, and abducted him. He brought the boy to Mount Olympus and made him cupbearer to the gods. This upset Hera, who had enough problems as it was with Zeus' heterosexual affairs. But Zeus made the boy immortal and paid his father for the lad by giving him horses in exchange. The myth was a Greek apology for the widespread practice of homosexuality between older men and young boys.

While Zeus' descent from heaven was to satisfy his lust, Tonatiuh, the Mexican sun-god, who was also pictured as an eagle, snatched up the souls of the heroic dead and brought them to the Mansions of the Sun—as Odin did in Scandinavian mythology.

According to Aztec legend Mexico City was founded on the spot where an eagle was seen holding a bleeding snake in its talons. Today the eagle

Zeus, eagle-formed, could not resist the boy, Ganymede,
Whom he clasped in his warm embrace.

Anonymous Greek Poem

and the snake are at the center of the national flag of Mexico.

The eagle as a symbol of Zeus and Odin became associated with imperial power and was used by Roman, Austrian, and Russian rulers as part of their heraldic devices. When the United States chose the bald eagle for the new nation's symbol, Benjamin Franklin disagreed, as he wrote in a letter to his daughter:

> *I wish that the bald eagle had not been chosen as the representative of our country; he is a bird of bad moral character; he does not get his living honestly; you may have seen him perched on some dead tree, where, too lazy to fish for himself, he watches the labor of the fishing hawk, and when that diligent bird has at length taken a fish, and is bearing it to his nest for the supper of his mate and young ones, the bald eagle pursues him and takes it from him.*

Franklin further described the bald eagle as a "rank coward." He preferred the turkey gobbler as a better choice for the national symbol because it was unique to this continent. Konrad Lorenz in *King Solomon's Ring* writes of the eagle: "I hate to shatter the fabulous illusions about this glorious bird, but I must adhere to the truth: all true birds of prey are, compared with passerines or parrots, extremely stupid creatures. This applies particularly to the golden eagle, 'the eagle' of our mountains and poets, which is one of the most stupid among them. . . ." Lorenz goes on to tell how he bought an imperial eagle that would not hunt and even refused to harm a rabbit. (How often man is upset when nature does not act in accord with his wishes!)

One ancient Irish tale would seem to verify the stupidity of the eagle. All the birds met together to decide who was to be king. The one who could fly the highest was to be named. With the contest about to begin, the wren, knowing the eagle to be the one who could fly the highest, perched on the eagle's tail.

The eagle, leaving all the other birds behind, said: "I am king of the birds!"

But the wren, darting up above the eagle, cried out, "You lie!" This so angered the eagle that when the two were coming down, he hit the wren with his wing. From that day the wren has never been able to fly higher than a hawthorn bush.

The eagle in mythology and folklore is a carrier of persons as well as of birds. In medieval romances Alexander the Great was escorted to the gates of the Garden of Eden by an eagle. Hiding himself near the nest he had waited until the youngest and strongest settled down. Then, after he jumped upon the eagle's back, the bird soared to heaven, carrying the king. To speed him along Alexander held a large piece of meat just out of the eagle's reach.

According to ancient folk belief every ten years the eagle would fly near the sun, then plunge into the sea where, moulting its feathers, it would renew its youth. Psalm 103 (4–5) mentions this belief:

> *Who redeemeth thy life from destruction;*
> *   who crowneth thee with lovingkindness and tender mercies;*
> *Who satisfieth thy mouth with good things;*
> *   so that thy youth is renewed like the eagle's.*

Spenser in *The Faerie Queene* presents the image of the eagle coming out of the sea after renewing its life:

> *At last she saw, where he upstarted brave*
> *Out of the well wherein he drenched lay:*
> *An eagle, fresh out of the ocean wave,*
> *Where he hath left his plumes all hory gray,*
> *And deckt himself with feathers youthly gay. . . .*

The eagle's rebirth made it fit into Christian symbolism. St. Jerome says the eagle is an ideal symbol for Christ's Ascension to heaven as well as for prayers rising to the heavens. Dante in *The Divine Comedy* calls the eagle the bird of God, and St. John the Evangelist is often portrayed as an eagle or with an eagle companion, since his gospel was considered by the Church Fathers the most elevated and spiritual of all four accounts. Yet not only the Christians found the eagle an appropriate symbol for spiritual flight. Nietzsche, the nineteenth-century German philosopher and despiser of Christianity in all its manifestations, chose the eagle as one of the companions of his Solitary Sage in *Thus Spake Zarathustra*. The other animal companion is the snake. Nietzsche calls the eagle and snake the "proudest and shrewdest among animals."

While the eagle symbolized Zeus, Odin, and Christ, the hawk was one of the birds sacred to Apollo in his role as diviner. The hawk was also sacred to Horus, Ra, Osiris, and Seker in Egyptian mythology, and its worship was universal throughout Egypt in predynastic times. The center of the cult of the Hawk-god was Hieraconopolis, or Hawk City. In Egyptian mythology the hawk, aside from being a sun-bird, was a symbol of the human soul when represented with a human head. The hawk was so sacred that if one were killed the punishment was death to the murderer. Sacred hawks were kept at public expense, and they would come to their keepers when called, catching pieces of raw meat thrown to them in full flight.

Horus, son of Osiris and lord of Upper and Lower Egypt, was a hawk-headed god. He avenged his father's death by killing Set, the evil brother of Osiris, but in the process lost his eye, which was restored by the god Thoth. The representation of the eye of Horus came to be one of the most popular religious symbols in Egypt.

The hawk is one of the main characters in what is believed to be among the earliest, if not the earliest, fable: *The Hawk and the Nightingale.* The tale is told in Aesop as well as in Hesiod's *Work and Days,* which was written in the eighth century B.C.

A nightingale was sitting aloft an oak tree singing to his heart's content when a hawk swooped down and seized him. The nightingale begged the hawk to let him go, saying that he wasn't big enough to satisfy the hawk's great hunger.

"I should be an idiot," replied the hawk, "if I let go of the food in my hands for some that is not even in sight," and he ate the nightingale.

The hawk earned his little nightingale in the nature of things, but the vulture in fact and in lore must depend on other animals to make the kill. It is unable, despite its size, to rip open the hides of animals and must wait for the carcass to decompose before it can eat it. It therefore was an appropriate symbol of Ares, the Greek god of war. The ancients believed that vultures followed the soldiers into battle, foretelling by certain signs the ones that were to die. As if to verify the old belief, before the Battle of Salamanca in July 1812, swarms of vultures were seen cruising over the armies of Wellington and Marmont. The vultures that swarmed around the dead were believed to be female—there were no males. To conceive, the female would turn back to the southwind, which impregnated her. After three years she gave birth.

The vulture's connection with death is also part of its identification with the Egyptian Mut, Great Mother-Goddess of the sky and wife of the god Ammon-Ra at Thebes. Her vulture headdress symbolized maternity. Since the vulture fed on dead bodies, it became related to the Earth Mother and death, according to Jung. Always closely allied to death, however, is resurrection. The Parsees, Persian descendants of exiles to India who retain the precepts of Zoroastrian worship, expose their dead in specially built towers of silence so vultures will consume the bodies, thus quickening the resurrection of the dead.

Western man, in opposition to the Zoroastrian belief, does all he can to preserve his body from decay, erecting air-tight monuments and filling his body with alien fluids. One explanation given for the care is that the body should be ready for the resurrection. Others, however, see it as a fear that the destruction of the body is the complete end of life. Still others see it as a means of making money from the grief of the living over their dead.

OWL, MAGPIE, AND PARROT

One day Jesus went into a baker's shop and asked for some bread. The mistress of the shop immediately put some dough in the oven.

"That is too much," cried the woman's daughter.

The girl went to the oven and reduced the amount by half. Not satisfied with that, she went back to the oven and reduced the dough again. But, the dough began to rise and rise in the oven, pushing open the doors and falling across the floor.

"Heugh, heugh, heugh," cried the girl owl-like, and at that very moment Jesus turned her into an owl.

This English legend from Gloucestershire was known throughout the British Isles, though the details often varied. Some versions have an angel or fairy visit the shop, thus removing any vindictiveness from Jesus' action in transforming the stingy girl.

Shakespeare was familiar with one version of the legend, since he has Ophelia say in *Hamlet* (IV.5): "They say the owl was a baker's daughter." To Shakespeare and many of his contemporaries the owl was a demonic bird. It was the "vile owl" in the poet's *Troilus and Cressida* (II.1) and the "obscure bird" in *Macbeth* (II.3).

Shakespeare's castigation of the owl goes back to medieval folklore where the owl signified night and all that was dark and ugly. By extension the bird was also used to symbolize the Jews who "lived in darkness" because, as

They say the owl was a baker's daughter.

Shakespeare: *Hamlet*

Christians explained, they refused to accept Christ's gospel. The medieval identification of the owl with demonic forces, however, found its base in Jewish folklore and Egyptian mythology.

Jewish folklore believed that Lilith, or She of the Night, the wife given to Adam before Eve in Jewish legend, flew about as a night owl, making off with children. Although Hebrew Scripture does not contain the Lilith legend, the Prophet Isaiah (34:11–15) chooses the owl as one of the demonic birds that will haunt the land of Edom.

The Jewish dislike of the bird was not isolated, since the Egyptian hieroglyph for owl symbolized death, night, cold, and passivity. The owl hieroglyph was also used to indicate the sun below the horizon as the sun crossed the sea of darkness in its daily journey.

The owl's connection with night is even more evident in Aztec mythology. Techlotl, the god of the Underworld, was symbolized by a night owl. With the Pimas, a southwestern Indian tribe in the United States, the owl was a symbol of the souls of the dead. If an owl happened to be hooting at the time of death, it was certain that the owl was waiting for the soul of the dying man. Owl feathers were always given to a dying person to help him into the next world. If a family had no owl feathers, they would obtain them from the tribe medicine man, who traditionally kept them in stock. Feathers from a freshly captured owl were best.

Greek and Roman mythology had different attitudes toward the owl, which affected the European outlook. The city of Athens had so many owls that the proverb "Taking owls to Athens" was an ancient equivalent of "Coals to Newcastle." The Romans, on the other hand, ritually purified Rome if one owl accidentally strayed into the capitol city.

The magpie, like the owl, is considered a bird of ill omen in European folklore. But it does possess some good qualities. The divergent attitude toward the magpie is expressed in this line rhyme from Lancashire, England, which runs:

> *One for sorrow*
> *Two for mirth*
> *Three for a wedding*
> *Four for a death.*

Some versions change the last line to "Four for a birth," expressing a more hopeful attitude toward the bird's omens. In Oriental folklore a magpie nesting near a house is a sign of good luck, and it is especially good to hear one just before you start a journey. The magpie, like the owl, is a soul-bird in some American Indian tales and in Teutonic folklore.

Neither good nor evil traits are assigned to the parrot, since the bird's voice, so close to man's, has received so much attention. Aristotle points out that the tongue of a parrot resembles that of a man, and parrots have been taught everything from Scripture verses to the most obscene language. An English clergyman came upon a talking parrot in a cage in Billingsgate, noted at the time for the obscene language of its inhabitants. The bird, an expert at the local vulgarisms, was moved to another street where it picked up the language of a coffee house. The worst it said there was "Bring a dish of toffy" or "What's the news?" The minister, feeling that the parrot's "conversion" was complete, took it back to its old home—and within a week it swore and cursed again with a vengeance.

Foul-mouthed or not, the parrot has been highly valued for its company and conversation. The Maharajah of Nawanagar had a parrot 115 years old who traveled with the ruler in a Rolls-Royce and even had an international passport. Everywhere the Maharajah went the bird was close by, rather like Mary's little lamb. This was not just a peculiarity of an Indian potentate, for George V of England kept a parrot perched upon his shoulders while he read state papers. Once when the king was ill, the bird became very sad until it was allowed into his company, when the cry "Bless my buttons! Bless my buttons! All's well" echoed through the palace.

RAVEN AND CROW

Coronis was a beautiful maiden loved by the god Apollo, who valued her chastity above all her other virtues. But the girl was not so chaste as the god imagined. The raven, Apollo's sacred bird in his role as god of prophecy, spied Coronis in the embraces of a young man. He flew in all haste to tell Apollo about the girl's infidelity. As the raven was speeding on his way, a crow followed him and asked where he was going in such a hurry.

"To inform Apollo of Coronis' infidelity," the raven said.

"Don't be a fool," the crow replied. "Listen to me and don't repeat the story, for the god doesn't want to hear it."

Not listening to the crow's advice—and forgetting that gods, like men, are loath to learn of their lovers' inconstancies—the raven continued on his way.

Finally he reached Apollo, and the first words out of his mouth were that Coronis was having sexual relations with a young mortal named Ischys. When the god heard, his laurel fell from his head, he turned pale, and began to swell with anger. Apollo took up his bow and shot his love—wounding her so that her white limbs were stained with blood.

"I am justly punished by you, Apollo," the girl cried, "but you not only kill me. You kill your child inside me."

While the body of Coronis was on the funeral pyre, Apollo snatched his son from her, who became Asklepius, the physician. Later Apollo rued his hasty shot and became infuriated with the raven who had brought him the news. He cursed the raven and turned the bird to black, for until then ravens had been white.

Apollo's transformation of the raven in the Greek myth is echoed in Jewish folklore. When Yahweh God put Noah into the Ark with his family and two of every beast, they were not to engage in any sexual intercourse— neither Noah, his wife, the sons and their wives, nor any of the animals. But after a time the raven just could not resist and yielded to the temptation, for which he was punished by being turned black.

Later Noah wished to send out the raven to see if the flood waters had abated, but the raven at first refused.

"How do I know you will let me back into the Ark?" asked the raven.

"You sinful creature," Noah cried. "You have been put among the unclean birds. You're not fit to eat or to sacrifice. If you don't go out, I'll throw you out and you'll be wiped off the face of the earth." Yahweh heard Noah's threat to the raven.

"Leave the raven alone," God called. "In days to come when Elijah the Prophet is near starvation, I will send ravens to feed him."

The raven then went out, but never returned to the Ark. Jewish folklore says he was eating the bodies of the dead that were floating in the waters. This motif of the raven who does not return is found in other mythologies.

Utnapishthim, the Babylonian Noah, also sent out a raven when his Ark came to rest on Mount Nisir. In the *Gilgamesh* epic, Utnapishthim sent out a dove, a swallow, and a raven. Since the raven did not return, Utnapishthim knew the waters had abated.

As Yahweh foretold, ravens fed the Prophet Elijah, according to the account in First Kings (17:6). Christianity adopted the Jewish Scriptural legend and applied it to some of its saints. A raven brought food to St. Paul the Hermit, who lived ninety-eight years in a cave. Each day the raven brought a loaf of bread and some dates. When St. Anthony the Abbot came to visit St. Paul, both were fed by ravens. The scene is often depicted in Western art.

Aside from bringing food, the raven was the guardian of the dead in

Christian folklore. The body of St. Vincent was guarded from intruders by a raven. This connection with the dead made the raven a natural symbol of the devil, and St. Benedict reported that the devil appeared to him in the form of a raven. A legend narrated in the *Koran* (Surah V) says a raven was scratching "the ground to show Cain how to hide his brother's body."

In Scandinavian mythology two ravens, Hugin, or Thought, and Muninn, or Memory, brought news to Odin of what happened during the day. As a result Odin was sometimes called the God of Ravens. The raven was also sacred to Hera, wife of Zeus, in her role as guardian of cities, and as said earlier, of Apollo as god of prophecy.

The ominous character of the raven is reflected in literature. Cassius in *Julius Caesar* (V.1) tells how the ravens

> *Fly o'er our heads and downward look on us*
> *As we were sickly prey. . . .*

reflecting the belief that the bird would "smell death" and was therefore a dreaded visitor.

Roman legend, however, tells a tale in which the raven alighted on the helmet of Valerius, a soldier, when he was about to fight a Gallic warrior. Valerius took this as a good sign and prayed to the gods to aid him in his fight. The gods heard the prayer, for the bird came again in the middle of the fray and plucked out the eyes of the warrior from Gaul, bringing victory to Valerius, who then took the surname Corvus after the bird. A Cornish legend says King Arthur still lives in the guise of a raven, and since one might be the great king, the bird is not killed.

In an Eskimo myth the Great Raven is the creator of animals and women. In an Athabascan legend the mighty raven Yetl, with eyes of fire, descended to earth and called forth animals. Quikinague or Jutkinnaku, the Big Raven, is the benevolent creator in Koryak mythology. Yet alongside this beneficent aspect lie the raven's greed and voraciousness, which are part of the North American Indian myths.

The crow, like the raven, fares poorly in European folklore. The English go so far as to say the crow visits hell at midsummer each year and makes a payment to the devil of its feathers. The birds do moult in midsummer, and since they are usually absent from their regular haunts during that time, it is easy for the superstition to prosper.

The Greek historian and moralist Plutarch uses the crow in one of his essays dealing with chastity—a subject that obsessed late Greek and early Christian writers. The crow is cited for its faithfulness to its mate because, according to Plutarch, it does not remarry for nine human generations.

"Can Penelope match that?" the moralistic Plutarch cries out.

NIGHTINGALE, ROBIN, CUCKOO, AND SWALLOW

On the night Jesus was born a small snuff-brown bird was in his little nest in a cave. The bird had used the cave for his home for some time. On Christmas night he was suddenly awakened by a bright light that drenched the whole cave, and with the light came the sound of angels' voices singing praises to God. Moved by the sweet voices, the bird joined in the heavenly song and became the first nightingale.

At the same time, a small bird whose nest was some way from the cave saw shepherds get up and leave their warm fire to go to the cave's entrance. The bird flew down to the fire to fan it with his wings. The flames soared higher and higher, casting their yellow-red light upon the bird as he flapped his wings. The color never left the robin.

These two European legends, found complete in Joseph Gaer's wonderful book *The Lore of the New Testament*, were popular explanations to account for the nightingale's song and the robin's colorful breast. In the legend the nightingale is identified as male, though most Western literature insists on identifying the singer as female. German uses the feminine gender for the nightingale, and Oscar Wilde's tale *The Nightingale and the Rose* also identifies the bird as female.

Crediting the female of the species with the lovely voice probably originated in the Greek myth of Philomela, who was turned into a nightingale.

Philomela was the daughter of Pandion, king of Athens. Her sister Procne was married to the king's ally, Tereus, king of Thrace, who was the son of the war-god Ares. Tereus sent a message to Pandion, saying his wife Procne was dead and asked that Philomela might be sent to him for his second wife. When Philomela arrived, the king raped her and cut out her tongue so she would not be able to tell of his crime. Procne, who had been away, returned to the palace and found a piece of embroidery on which Philomela had woven her story. Procne took her revenge on her evil husband by killing their child Itys and serving him to the king. When the king discovered the slaughter, he pursued the woman. The gods, having watched this tragedy long enough, turned him into a hoopoe, Philomela into a nightingale, and Procne into a swallow. (This telling of the tale is based on a Latin source, since the earlier Greek version has Procne turned into the nightingale. The Latin version is the one, however, that has left its mark on Western literature.)

The gruesome fate of Philomela makes the nightingale's identification with death seem almost plausible. Keats in his "Ode to a Nightingale" uses the bird for such a purpose, while Hans Christian Andersen in his magnificent fairy tale *The Nightingale* has the bird bargain with death to save the Chinese emperor's life.

The emperor had cast aside a real nightingale for a mechanical one, but when he lay on his death bed, no one was near to wind up the mechanical bird. Death stared with his great hollow eyes at the emperor. Then there was a sound at the window and suddenly a lovely song. The live nightingale had heard of the emperor's sad plight and had come to sing to him of comfort and hope. As it sang the spectre grew paler and paler, the blood ran quicker through the emperor's weak limbs. Even Death listened to the beautiful song, saying: "Sing, little nightingale, more."

"But will you give me that splendid golden sword? Will you give me that rich banner? Will you give me the emperor's crown?" cried the nightingale.

All these had been taken from the emperor by Death, and Death gave up each of these treasures for a song. The nightingale sang on of the quiet churchyard where the white roses grow, where the elder blossom smells sweet, and where the fresh grass is moistened by the tears of survivors. Then

Death felt a longing to see this garden and floated out of the window in the form of a cold white mist.

Andersen's tale provides the plot for Stravinsky's opera *The Nightingale*, as well as for his subsequent symphonic poem *The Song of the Nightingale*, based on music from the opera. The theme of the mechanical bird is harsh, dissonant music; that of the real bird is just the opposite.

In reality a nightingale's song is not meant to please either humans or other birds. It is a warning to all other male nightingales to stay out of the singer's territory—as well as an invitation to the females to join the male.

The cuckoo, unlike the nightingale, has a reputation in folklore for considerable sexual attraction. Both Indra, the ancient Hindu sky-god, and the Greek Zeus chose the form of the cuckoo for wooing women. The Romans used to call an adulterer a "cuckoo," while Shakespeare has a little song in *Love's Labour's Lost* (V.2) that sums up the matter quite well:

> *The cuckoo then on every tree,*
> *Mocks married men; for thus sings he,*
>   *"Cuckoo!*
> *Cuckoo, cuckoo!" O word of fear,*
> *Unpleasing to a married ear!*

The cuckoo's sexual reputation comes from its identification with being the herald of spring, the season of rebirth. The swallow also has been chosen as a harbinger of spring. In Christian lore it is a symbol of the Incarnation and Resurrection of Christ, since the bird disappears in winter and reappears in spring. Many paintings of the Nativity depict a swallow nesting under the eaves, while some works portraying the Crucifixion have a swallow hovering above the cross and offering Christ consolation. Hence the name "bird of consolation" for the swallow.

The sentimental aspect of the swallow is missing in a Jewish folktale that credits the bird with a good deal of cleverness.

One year after creation Yahweh God called all living creatures together to ask if they were pleased with their lot. Everyone replied affirmatively except for Adam.

"The snake is forever near me," Adam said, "and I never have a moment's rest. Why don't you do away with him?"

"The snake was here before you," Yahweh said. "But to satisfy you I will banish him from your door."

"If you do that," said the snake, "I will starve to death."

"No," said Yahweh, "you shall feed on the best food in the world."

Now all the plants and animals were very upset, since they might be chosen the best food in the world. Yahweh then said he would create an animal who would taste all the foods of the earth for one year and return with a report on which was the best. So Yahweh created the gnat and sent him on the mission.

A year later when the gnat was on his way to report to Yahweh, he met the swallow.

"What is the best food in the world!" the swallow asked.

"Man's blood is the best food," replied the gnat.

"What did you say?" said the swallow as he came closer to the gnat.

"Man—" the gnat called out, his mouth wide open.

In a flash the swallow's beak tore out the gnat's tongue. When the gnat appeared before Yahweh, all he could say was *"Tzzzz–Tzzzz."*

"If I may speak," said the swallow to Yahweh. "Just before the gnat lost his power of speech, he told me the most tasty food was a frog."

"So," said Yahweh, "the snake shall live on the frog."

Then all creation left the presence of Yahweh, and the swallow, looking down on the snake, said: "You thought you would live off man but instead you have only a frog."

With that the snake leaped up and caught the swallow by his tail. The swallow escaped, but not before it lost some of his feathers. That is why the swallow has a forked tail. Ever since it is the duty of man to leave food on the Sabbath for the swallow so he does not know hunger.

PEACOCK, WOODPECKER, PARTRIDGE, AND GOLDFINCH

Golden, the king of the wild ducks, had a beautiful daughter whom he loved very much and to whom he promised to grant every wish she desired. When the duck-princess was old enough to marry, she asked her father for the right to choose her own husband.

"That's unheard of," said the king, "but I have given my word and a king cannot take back his word."

All the birds in the kingdom came before the princess. There were wild ducks, eagles, swans, owls, parrots, storks, plovers, ostriches, and cockatoos —in short, every type of bird in the kingdom. They all began to march before her, but only the peacock, with his dazzling plumage, caught her attention.

"I wish the peacock for my husband," said the princess to her father.

So the king announced the decision, and the peacock, overjoyed, spread his feathers, began to dance, and sang in a most disagreeable tone.

This lack of modesty upset the princess, who ran to her father and said she had changed her mind. She did not wish to marry such a vain bird as the peacock. The king smiled at his daughter and said he would pick a husband for her. And when he did, he chose another wild duck. (A stick-to-your-own-kind moral.)

This Buddhist tale displays one of the most common beliefs regarding the peacock: its phenomenal vanity. The peacock is often pictured in literature as a proud and vain fool, as in Shakespeare's *Henry VI, Part I* (III.3):

> *Let frantic Talbot triumph for a while*
> *And like a peacock sweep along his tail;*
> *We'll pull his plumes and take away his train. . . .*

Perhaps because of its legendary vanity and arrogance the Romans saw the peacock as a symbol of princesses, as they did the eagle of princes. Royalty was not ashamed of being proud or vain.

The origin of the peacock's pride, its richly colored tail feathers with its "eyes," is described in a Greek myth. Hera, the wife of Zeus, sent the hundred-eyed giant Argos to watch Io, a mistress of Zeus who had been transformed into a heifer. Zeus, in the guise of a woodpecker, led the god Hermes to slay the giant. Hera, who could punish neither of the gods, contented herself with taking the giant's eyes and placing them in the tail of her favorite bird.

In Christian symbolism the peacock's tail was sometimes used as the "all-seeing eye" of the Church, which was intended as a loving image, but actually captured the often Inquisitorial tone of the Church. In Christian lore the peacock symbolized immortality of the soul. It was believed, for instance, that peacock flesh did not decay. St. Augustine writes in his massive work *The City of God:* "Who except God, the Creator of all things, endowed the flesh of the dead peacock with the power of never decaying?" Legend says the saint experimented with the bird and found this to be true.

The paintings in early Christian catacombs often show two peacocks facing each other, depicting the souls of the faithful drinking from the Fountain of Life. Moslem legend says the peacock was originally the guardian of the Gates to Paradise—but it ate the devil who then, inside the bird, entered Paradise and could work the Fall of Adam and Eve.

Zeus was transformed into a woodpecker in the story of Io, as was the sky-god Indra in Hindu mythology and Mars in Roman mythology. Partly because of its connection with these pagan gods the early Christians identified the bird with the devil, though the woodpecker's association with the approach of winter, a time of death, may have also influenced the Christian attitude. Today the nearest we come to the demonic woodpecker is Woody the Woodpecker in the popular animated cartoons, though perhaps his antics fit more into the role of the trickster.

The partridge shares with the woodpecker a demonic nature. For the Christian the bird was a living example of "perverted" sexual habits because, according to one twelfth-century Latin bestiary, the males coupled with other male birds. The female partridge did not escape condemnation either, since she was believed to steal the eggs of other birds. This belief is found in a verse of Jeremiah (17:11):

> *As the partridge sitteth on eggs, and hatcheth them not;*
> *so he that getteth riches, and not by right,*
> *shall leave them in the midst of his days,*
> *and at his end shall be a fool.*

St. Ambrose, knowing this verse in Jeremiah, plainly called the partridge the devil. Yet in an early apocryphal Christian work, *The Acts of John,* the bird is the soul of the faithful. The Christian author obviously was not aware of the sexual habits of the bird, since the Early Church considered such deviant sexual behavior worthy of hell.

Thus it is easy to see that the woodpecker and the partridge are in the devil's camp. The goldfinch, however, escaped such condemnation because, according to Christian legend, it was fond of eating thistles and thorns— symbols of the Passion of Christ. Often one finds a Renaissance painting of a Madonna and Child where the babe is holding a goldfinch in his hands, indicating his future suffering on the Cross.

One wishes, however, that the goldfinch had been chosen as a beneficent symbol for a reason other than its masochistic habits.

DOVE

Since God had blessed Joachim and Anna with a child, they dedicated the girl Mary to the service of the Lord in the Temple of Jerusalem. Mary lived in the Temple and was educated by a dove, which descended to her every day and taught her about God. The girl's food was supplied by an angel. When Mary was twelve years old, the priests met in council.

"Mary can no longer stay in the Temple," they said. "She is no longer a girl but a woman. If she stays she will defile the sacred place, since blood now issues from her."

Zacharias, the high priest, then went to the Altar of the Lord to ask what should be done with Mary, as the girl had taken a vow of virginity. (A very unusual detail, since such a vow would be contrary to the Jewish practices of the day.) Suddenly an angel of the Lord came to him.

"Zacharias," he said, "go and call all the widowers among the people to come to the Temple. Each one should bring his staff, and by a sign from heaven the Lord will choose the one he wants to marry the virgin."

News went out, and all the widowers came to Jerusalem. Joseph, who was a carpenter, put down his tools and made his way to the Temple with his staff. The high priest took the staffs of all the men and went into the Holy of Holies once more to ask God which one was to be chosen. Then he came out and gave the staffs back to the men. Joseph was the last one to receive his, and when the high priest handed it to him, a dove came out of it and flew upon the head of Joseph. (In Egypt the staffs of the gods were phallic symbols.)

"You have been chosen to be the husband of Mary," the high priest told Joseph the carpenter.

"But I am old and have children," said Joseph. The Lord, however, had chosen Joseph and he took the girl to be his wife.

This Christian legend is found in the *Protevangelion*, an apocryphal gospel that circulated in the Early Church and was said to have been written by St. James the Less.

In another apocryphal gospel the dove descended from heaven to rest upon the staff of Joseph, indicating he was to be the husband. In one legend Joachim and Anna, parents of the Virgin, dreamed of a dove before her birth. In the canonical gospel accounts of the Baptism of Christ a dove descended. And in the gospel of Mark (1:9–11) we have:

> *And it came to pass in those days, that Jesus came from Nazareth of Galilee, and was baptized of John in Jordan. And straightway coming up out of the water, he saw the heavens opened, and the Spirit like a dove descending upon him: And there came a voice from heaven, saying, Thou art my beloved Son, in whom I am well pleased.*

From these various accounts in Scripture and legend the dove came to symbolize the Holy Spirit in Christian art. Even today some Russian Orthodox believers refuse to eat the bird because of its identification with the Holy Spirit. Since the Holy Spirit inspires evangelists, the bird is often shown with saints noted for their writings, such as the sixth-century Pope Gregory the Great. The Moslems also have a belief that the dove is the Holy Spirit. According to one legend a dove used to feed out of the ear of Mohammed, and his followers believed it was the Holy Spirit giving the Prophet advice. Shakespeare asks in *Part I, Henry VI,* (I.2):

> *Was Mahomet inspired with a dove?*

If Shakespeare found the Moslem belief difficult to accept, he was merely portraying the prejudice of his age, since the Bible has the Spirit of

God moving "upon the face of the waters" in Genesis (1:2), indicating that God was thought of as a hovering bird. The Mandayan creation legend from the Philippines says a dovelike bird laid two eggs, one at the source of a river, whence came woman, the other at the mouth of a river, whence came man. In the familiar account of the Flood in Genesis (8:8–12) it was a dove that told Noah the waters had abated. The Greek mythological account of the Flood has Deucalion, the Greek Noah, releasing a dove from the ark. If she came back, it would be a sign that the rains had not stopped; if she flew away, it would show fair weather coming. Pigeons and doves were the only birds that could be offered in sacrifice in Leviticus (1:14), serving as substitutes by poor people who could not offer more expensive animals to placate God.

Aside from Christianity's use of the dove as a symbol of the Holy Spirit, the bird came also to symbolize the souls of the faithful. Numerous saints' legends tell of the soul of the departing saint leaving the body in the form of a dove—for example, St. Scholastica, sister of St. Benedict, and St. Reparata, an earlier Palestinian saint. The Christian belief is found in earlier mythological concepts. In the *Iliad*, for instance, doves were hung from the mast of a ship and shot at during the funeral games for the dead Patroclus, the lover of Achilles. This belief in soul-birds is still held in certain parts of Great Britain, as well as in Slavic countries.

While the dove symbolizes the Holy Spirit and purity, it is also the source of the Virgin's conception of Christ, giving the bird a phallic symbolism as well. Other mythologies reflect the same belief. Astarte and Aphrodite, two great goddesses who originate in the Great Mother-Goddess, had doves sacrificed to them in their temples. One Greek myth tells of the origin of the doves that drew the chariot of the love-goddess Aphrodite. Eros and Aphrodite were picking flowers in a contest to see who could pick the most. Eros was winning when a nymph sided with the goddess. Becoming indignant, Eros changed the nymph into a dove. Aphrodite, in sympathy with the nymph, chose the dove as her symbol. Doves, therefore, drew the chariot of the goddess.

Today the dove is best known as a peace sign used by people of nearly every political persuasion. Picasso's dove has been reproduced and repeated so often on banners, posters, and stickers that it is a cliché. The following anecdote is offered to counter the sentimental modern view of the dove.

The poet Wordsworth and his sister were walking in a country lane when they heard a stock dove cooing. A farmer's wife passed by and talking to herself, said: "Oh, I do like stock doves." Dorothy Wordsworth, beaming with joy that the woman had such poetry in her, was deeply touched. But the old woman continued her sentence: "Some like them in a pie. For my part, there's nothing like 'em stewed in onions!"

COCK

An English squire sold his soul to the devil with the condition that after his death the fiend would also have the squire's skin. All went well for the squire, but then the day of death drew near, so he called a friend and told him the story. He asked that his friend be present when the devil came for the flaying. The friend granted the deathbed wish, but later realized what he had agreed to. In despair he went to the local parson to ask what to do, since he could not break his promise to the dying man. The parson, a man knowledgeable in devil lore, told the friend to take a cock with him to the cemetery for protection against the devil's wiles. The man went to the graveyard, cock under arm, and waited for the devil. Exactly at midnight the devil arrived, opened the grave, took the corpse from the coffin, and flayed it. When the devil had concluded, he looked at the skin and said: "Well, it wasn't worth the trouble after all. It's filled with holes."

Suddenly the cock under the arm of the friend began to crow. "If that bird were not with you," the devil cried out, "I would take your skin right off your back before you died!"

But the devil could not bear the sound of the cock's crowing and fled, leaving the man trembling but safe.

The belief that at cock-crow all the evil spirits that haunt the night must flee is widespread in European folklore. It is mentioned by the early Chris-

And sounding in advance its victory,
My song jets forth so clear, so proud, so preemptory,
That the horizon, seized with a rosy trembling,
Obeys me.

Edmond Rostand: *Chantecler*

tian poet Prudentius in one of his hymns and repeated in a hymn ascribed
to St. Ambrose:

> *Hark; for chanticleer is singing,*
> *Hark! he chides the lingering sun.*
> *And the morning star replies*
> *And lets loose the imprisoned day;*
> *And the godless bandit flees*
> *From his haunt and from his prey.*

The shrill crow of the cock (*cock-a-doodle-doo* to the English; *co-co-ri-co*
to the French) announces the rising sun. Thus the Greeks easily identified
the bird with Apollo in his role as sun-god. Shakespeare in *Hamlet* (I.1)
refers to the cock as "the trumpet to the morn," and the English poet
Thomas Gray, less taken with the sound, calls it a "shrill clarion." In either
case it was believed strong enough to dispel all ghosts—both good and bad
—from the earth, for at daybreak they had to return to their own haunts.
Shakespeare in *Hamlet* (I.1) also alludes to the belief that the cocks crow
all night on Christmas Eve so as to drive away every malignant spirit and
evil influence. Marcellus, speaking of the ghost of Hamlet's father, says:

> *It faded on the crowing of the cock.*
> *Some say that ever, 'gainst that season comes*
> *Wherein our Saviour's birth is celebrated,*
> *The bird of dawning singeth all night long;*
> *And then, they say, no spirit dare stir abroad,*
> *The nights are wholesome, then no planets strike,*
> *No fairy takes, nor witch hath power to charm,*
> *So hallow'd and so gracious is that time.*

The cock's role as announcer of the dawn made it an appropriate Christian symbol for the Resurrection of Christ. The cock became one of the
most popular decorations for the tops of church buildings because of its
ability to frighten demons when it announced the sunrise. One Christian
legend widespread in Ireland tells of the soldiers guarding the tomb of
Christ, who were boiling a cock for breakfast. Discussing whether Jesus

would rise from the tomb or not, one soldier laughed at the whole idea.

"He will no more rise from the tomb," he said, "than this cock will get up out of the pot."

Immediately the cock jumped up out of the pot and crowed—and shortly after, Christ came out of the tomb.

In Christian legend, however, the cock is more usually known for its role in Peter's denials of Jesus as narrated in the Gospels. Jesus predicted that Peter would deny that he knew him and Peter protested, saying he would never deny his master. But later as Peter watched Jesus taken before the tribunal, a maidservant questioned him and he denied knowing Jesus. Then, warming himself before a fire, he denied Jesus a second time. When questioned again if he were a follower of Jesus, Peter stoutly said "No"—and then the cock crowed. The words of Jesus came back to Peter: "Before the cock crow, thou shalt deny me thrice" (Matthew 26:75). Peter wept bitterly at what he had done, and many paintings of the saint portray him with the cock nearby as one of his symbols.

The story of Peter's denials is one of the most realistic accounts in the Gospels, but another version, not in the New Testament but in a spurious gospel, has a fantastic air about it. When Jesus was in the house of Simon the Leper, a cock was being prepared for Jesus and his disciples for dinner. Before they could eat, Judas ran out of the house. Jesus told the roasted cock to follow Judas, and the cock left the platter and ran after the apostle. Later the cock returned to tell Jesus of Judas' betrayal. As a reward Jesus immediately sent the bird to heaven.

Many mythologies have a high regard for the cock. He was associated with the Greek goddess Demeter and her daughter Persephone as a symbol of fertility. Cocks were often used in sacrifices to the gods. Sometimes a cock could be substituted for a human victim, as in Aztec ceremonies. Cocks were also sacrificed by the Romans, as they were sacred to Mars, the wargod, because of their fighting nature. But they were also sacred to Asklepius, the god of medicine, along with the snake, for their curative properties. Cocks formed part of a good many ancient medicinal recipes; they are used in voodoo ceremonies simultaneously as sacrificial and curative creatures. In marriage ceremonies among southern Slavs and in Hungary the bridegroom carries a cock or its image. He also has a wooden cock carved upon his house or put on the roof to guarantee a happy and fertile sex life.

BEE, BUTTERFLY, AND BEETLE

The handsome hero Lemminkainen was sent by the Mistress of Pohjola to kill the swan floating upon the River of Death. Lying in wait for the hero, however, was a cowherd who killed Lemminkainen and then cut his body into pieces, throwing them into the river. Soon afterward blood began to trickle from Lemminkainen's hairbrush at his home, and his mother knew at once that death had overtaken her beloved son. Distraught, she traveled until she came to the River of Death and picked out all the pieces of her son's body. Then she put the pieces together through magic incantations, but as yet the body had no life in it.

She called upon a bee to fetch honey for her son, saying:

> *O thou bee, thou bird of honey,*
> *King of all the woodland flowerets,*
> *Go thou forth to fetch me honey,*
> *Go thou forth to seek for honey . . .*
> *As an ointment for the patient,*
> *And so quite restore the sick one.*

The bee heard the words of Lemminkainen's mother and went to the meadows, sucked the honey from the tips of six bright flowers, and rushed back to the River of Death. When the salve did not work, the bee was sent out to gather more, but again it did not work. After the third journey the mother anointed her beloved son, saying:

> *Rise, my son, from out thy slumber,*
> *From thy dreams do thou awaken,*
> *From this place so full of evil,*
> *And a resting-place unholy.*

Lemminkainen was restored to life and went on to numerous other adventures, which form part of the Finnish epic poem *The Kalevala*, or *Land of Heroes*. (Lemminkainen's restoration to life forms one part of Sibelius' *Four Legends for Orchestra*. The Finnish epic also influenced the meter of Longfellow's poem *Hiawatha*.)

Honey as a life restorative was a widespread belief in many mythologies. In East Russia the Tchuwashes worshiped a bee-god and drank beer sweetened with honey at the sacred festivals. In Greek mythology Zeus was sometimes called *Melissaios* or Bee-man, from the legend that he had a son by a nymph who, fleeing the wrath of Hera, Zeus' wife, hid their child in the woods, where his father sent him food by the bees. The bee also served as a symbol of Artemis in her role as orgiastic nymph, and was identified with Demeter in Greek and with Cybele in Roman mythology as a sign of productivity and life. Vishnu, Krishna, and Indra in Hindu mythology are called *Madhava*, or nectar-born ones, and are often portrayed with a bee resting on a lotus flower. Karma, the Hindu god of love, has a bowstring made up of bees.

Egyptians used honey not only as a sweetener for their cakes, but also in their mummification process. Babylonians and Sumerians offered honey to their gods at religious ceremonies.

According to an Aesop fable man's great desire for the bees' product upset one queen bee. She went up to Mount Olympus, the home of the gods, and offered honey to Zeus. The god was delighted with the offering and promised to give the queen bee whatever she wished.

"Give me a sting that will kill anyone who tries to take my honey," said the queen bee.

The request angered Zeus, who preferred men to bees, but he said: "You shall have your wish—but it will cost you your life. Every time a bee stings a man the bee will remain in the wound and die."

Notwithstanding Aesop's selfish bee, the Orphics, a mystical religious sect, said the bee symbolized the human soul, since it produced sweet honey, and bees swarmed around their hives as souls around the Divine Unity.

Christianity adopted some of the mythological symbolism of the bee for its own legends. St. John Chrysostom, or Golden-Mouthed, was born with a swarm of bees hovering around his mouth, according to legend, to symbolize the sweetness of his preaching. The same story was told of St. Ambrose as well as of St. Bernard of Clairvaux, both noted preachers. In fact Ambrose compared the beehive to the Church and the bee to a diligent Christian. His belief in the bee's diligence came from the story that bees never sleep but are continually working.

The Christian moral attitude toward the work of bees is best summed up in a letter St. Jerome wrote: "Make hives for bees. . . . Watch the creatures and learn how to run a monastery and control a kingdom!" Jerome, well known for his harsh words on the subject of female sexuality, made no note of the fact that the ruler of the bees was a female.

Aside from the bees' administrative abilities, they were also believed to be excellent soldiers. Gobnait, an Irish saint of the sixth century, let loose a hive of bees against invading chiefs in her district. The bees attacked the eyes of the soldiers, causing them to flee. This folk motif is also found in numerous Danish, English, and German folktales, as well as in Jewish and Japanese ones.

The origin of bees naturally interested many minds, since the insect was so valuable. German Christians held that bees were created by God to supply wax for church candles, while a Breton belief said bees were created from the tears of Christ on the cross. The Breton belief ultimately goes back to Egypt where Ra, the sun-god, produced bees from his tears.

The most common myth about the origin of bees, however, was that they were produced from the carcasses of dead oxen. The fact that the skeleton rib cage of the ox provided a perfect natural framework for a wild beehive seemed proof to the ancients that bees originated there. Virgil devotes the second half of his *Fourth Georgie*, which is entirely concerned with bees, to this belief that bees were produced from decaying oxen. The idea was no poetical fancy on Virgil's part, since it was held by Aristotle and his numerous descendants, both philosophical and scientific, well into the seventeenth century.

Along with the common belief of the origin of bees went the superstition that bees had to be informed of the death of their keeper, or they would leave or die. In Mark Twain's *Huckleberry Finn* Jim tells Huck: "If a man owned a beehive and the man died, the bees must be told it before sun-up next morning, or else the bees would all weaken down and quit work and die." This belief perhaps originates from the earlier myth that bees were the messengers of gods, announcing the arrival of the dead in the Underworld.

The butterfly is sometimes used as a sign of the Resurrection of Christ, but more often as a symbol of the general resurrection of the dead. The butterfly's natural history lends itself ideally to this symbolism. It is a caterpillar, a chrysalis, and then a butterfly—Life, Death, and Resurrection. Some mystical groups, however, such as the Gnostics, looked upon the butterfly as a symbol of corrupt flesh. The Angel of Death in Gnostic art was portrayed crushing a butterfly. In Slavic countries it was believed that butterflies, symbols of the soul, issued from the mouths of witches to invade living bodies when the true soul was absent.

The beetle or scarab served as a resurrection symbol for Ra, the sun-god in Egyptian mythology. Egyptian beetles lay their eggs in the sand, roll them up in a tiny ball of manure, and then propel them along the ground— exactly as the sun rolled across the heavens in Egyptian mythology. Irish Christians, however, not having the Egyptian cosmology, looked upon the *darbhodaol*, a species of long black beetle, as a devil that ate the souls of sinners. If, for instance, one accepted money from the devil, a *darbhodaol* would be found in the hand instead. Yet Irish reapers would sometimes put a beetle in the handle of their tools, believing it would speed up their work. Obviously, the devil had some beneficent uses in Irish folklore.

BAT AND FLY

A great war was about to start between the birds and the land animals—and the bat had to decide which side he would join.

"Come with us," cried some birds perched in the treetops.

The bat replied: "I'm a land animal."

Later on, some of the land animals called out to the bat: "Come join us," but the bat replied: "I'm a bird."

Just as the war was about to begin, peace overtures were accepted on both sides and the battle was called off. The animals went back to celebrate the peace. When the bat tried to join the birds in their festivities, they turned against him and he had to flee. He then went to the land animals but soon had to beat a retreat or they would have torn him to pieces.

"I can see," said the bat, "that he who is not one thing or another has no true friends."

Aesop's fable reflects the ambiguous attitude man has long held for the nocturnal flying mammal. Its furry body, leatherlike wings, and sharp teeth make the bat an ideal demonic image in folklore. Sicilian peasants believe, for example, that the bat is the devil incarnate. They call the bat taddarita, and when they catch one, it is either burned over a candle or crucified. The Arabs do the same to keep away locusts, and the ancient Greeks and Romans used parts of the bat as amulets. Some cultures believe bats, like mice, contain the souls of the dead, and thus the bat is respected and feared. On the Ivory Coast of West Africa there is an island overrun with bats that are held sacred by the people. They will not kill the bats because they believe them to hold the souls of the dead. The Guatemalans used to worship a bat-god, Camazotz, who was much dreaded by the people because he had vampire brothers.

The existence of vampire bats that attack animals and humans served to color people's fears even further. The bat's identification with vampires has been impressed upon generations of moviegoers by the 1931 film of Bram Stoker's Victorian novel *Dracula*, in which Count Dracula spread his black cape and was transformed into a bat before the viewers' eyes. Germany produced the first film version of Stoker's novel in 1923, and it turned out to be gruesomely close to reality. Fritz Haarmann, called the "Hanover Vampire," killed at least twenty-seven young men between twelve and eighteen years of age by biting them in the neck, just as the vampire in the film and legend. Haarmann would haunt train stations and pick up a youngster by inviting him to his rooms. After feeding his victim, Haarmann would murder him, sell the clothes in his shop, and cut up the body, using some parts for food and throwing the rest in the river. Haarmann was convicted and decapitated in 1925. The judge's choice of execution accorded with folklore, decapitation being one of the surest ways to rid a land of vampires.

The idea that vampires may exist still fascinates many. In 1967 Roman Polanski filmed *The Fearless Vampire Killers*, supposedly a satire on the whole legend which nevertheless projected a macabre and frightening air. Richard Matheson's novel *I Am Legend* tells of a world inhabited by vampires with only one man left untouched by the fiends.

In contrast to the general Western concept of the diabolical nature of the bat (notwithstanding Batman and Robin of cartoon fame), the Orientals see the bat as a symbol of good luck. The Chinese symbol of the Five Bats indicates wealth, health, love of virtue, old age, and natural death. To insure all these blessings the Chinese eat bats. In Samoa the war-god Sepi Malosi, a large bat, flew before the victorious war party toward the one that was to be defeated.

Only the diabolical attributes of the bat are applied to the fly. Beelzebub symbolizes the devil or one of his main cohorts in Christian and Jewish

...Beelzebub the prince of the devils.

Matthew 12:24

folklore. Originally Beelzebub may have been a Syrian god called Baalze-bub, or Lord Bal, mentioned in Second Kings (1:3), whom the Hebrews mocked by deliberately calling Lord of Flies. One designation of the Greek Zeus was "he who wards off flies," indicating that meat dedicated to the god would be protected from devouring flies.

Beelzebub had many offspring in medieval Christian and Jewish folklore. One fly-demon, the offspring of Beelzebub and a nun, stung King Cunibert of Lombardy while the king was discussing how to rid the land of two evil counselors. The king's soldiers chased the fly-demon and succeeded in cutting off one of his legs. Later in the day, two noblemen whom the king wished to arrest were approached by a one-legged man who warned them of the plot. The evil counselors fled, saving their lives.

Thou art like the harpy,
Which, to betray, dost with thine angel's face,
Seize with thine eagle's talons.

Shakespeare: *Pericles*

PART FOUR
Animals of the Mind

UNICORNS

In James Thurber's *Fables for Our Times* there is a short tale of a man who told his wife that he had seen a unicorn in his garden. She informed the authorities. When they arrived the husband was out, and while they waited, the woman insisted that her husband had said he saw a unicorn. The husband returned, and they asked him if he had seen a unicorn in the garden. He replied: "Of course not! The unicorn is a mythical beast!" So the authorities carted off his wife to the madhouse. End of fable, with Thurber's moral: "Don't count your boobies before they're hatched."

Though Thurber's fable is about man-woman relationships, it is interesting to us that he chose the unicorn. It is the imaginary beast that continues to capture man's imagination as it did in earlier ages. The general iconography so well illustrated in the Unicorn Tapestry at The Cloisters in New York City shows a white horselike animal with a single horn about three feet long protruding from the middle of its forehead. This iconographic version of the animal, however, is not the only one. Pliny says the unicorn's body resembles a horse, its head a stag, its feet an elephant, its tail a boar, while its horn is black.

The unicorn's horn was its most valuable possession, since it was believed to be able to cure everything from epilepsy to poisoning. One reputed unicorn horn was kept in water in the Cathedral of St. Denis in France. It was so potent that even the water could cure the sick. An Italian who visited

England early in the reign of Henry VIII, commenting upon the riches of the religious houses and monasteries, wrote: "And I have been informed that, amongst other things, many of the monasteries possess unicorns' horns of an extraordinary size." Queen Elizabeth I, James I, and Charles I all had unicorn horns listed in the inventories of their possessions. The Great Elizabeth's was valued at a phenomenal £100,000.

Monasteries and royalty were not the only seekers of the unicorn's horn. Apothecaries until the eighteenth century powdered them to mix into drugs. Since there was no such horn, all sorts of horns were substituted, usually the entire tusk of a narwhal.

Even though the unicorn did not exist, folklore evolved a method for capturing one. A virgin was put in a field to lure the animal to her. This she accomplished by exposing her breasts. The animal, unable to resist such purity, would come up to the virgin, lie down, and, placing its head on her lap, fall asleep. The hunters could then trap the beast. In T. H. White's novel of King Arthur's life, *The Once and Future King*, three young boys tied a servant girl to a tree in hopes of catching a unicorn for their mother:

> *The unicorn went up to Meg the kitchenmaid, and bowed his head in front of her. He arched his neck beautifully to do this, and the pearl horn pointed to the ground at her feet, and he scratched in the heather with his silver hoofs to make a salute. . . . he went down first on one knee and then on the other till he was bowing in front of her. He looked up at her from this position, with his melting eyes, and at last laid his head upon her knee. He stroked his flat, white cheek against the smoothness of her dress, looking at her beseechingly. The whites of his eyes rolled with an upward flash. He settled his hind quarters coyly, and lay still, looking up. His eyes brimmed with trustfulness, and he lifted his near fore in a gesture of pawing.*

The gorgeous animal, however, was not long for this earth. White goes on to describe how the unicorn was slaughtered, making of the scene in the novel almost an account of the Passion of Christ. The symbolism is not outrageous, since the animal was often used in medieval imagery as a sign of

Christ's Incarnation. Just as the world destroyed Christ, so it destroys his image, the unicorn.

The identification of the unicorn with Christ, however, upset the members of the Council of Trent of the Roman Catholic Church held in the sixteenth century. They forbade its use as a symbol of Christ's Incarnation, though it was still retained as a sign of chastity.

It is not known whether the prelates came to their decision through scientific inquiry (the animal did not really exist) or thought the animal an inappropriate symbol for Christ, since in one legend, narrated by Leonardo da Vinci in his bestiary, the unicorn was captured by a virgin as a result of its own lustful advances.

The Church Fathers therefore thought it was best to remove the animal from Church symbolism. There was one problem, however, in their decision. They could not remove all the references to the animal in the Bible. When the Hebrew Bible was translated into Greek (the Septuagint), the translators took the Hebrew word *reem*, which might stand for a wild ox, and translated it *monokeros*, or one-horned. This rendering was followed in later Latin versions, which in turn influenced English translations such as the King James Version. In the Book of Numbers (23:22) we have the verse:

> *God brought them out of Egypt;*
> *he hath as it were the strength of an unicorn.*

The *Revised Standard Version* substituted "wild ox" in the verse.

One Jewish folktale said the unicorn had perished in the Great Flood, since it was too large to enter Noah's Ark. But another tale argued that God never destroys his own creation; if the unicorn was too large, then it would swim behind the Ark.

The unicorn obviously did swim behind the Ark, for it was continually engaged in combat with the lion, its arch-enemy in medieval lore. If a lion spotted a unicorn, it would run behind a tree. The unicorn, spotting its enemy, would then make a mad dash for the lion but in the process get its horn stuck in the tree. The lion would then come round and kill the unicorn. The fact that the unicorn and the lion were both symbols of Christ did not seem to bother the medieval imagination.

One nineteenth-century explanation for the rivalry of the unicorn and lion was that it preserved the ancient belief in the rivalry between the sun (the lion) and the moon (the unicorn). As the sun sets it seems to flee from the oncoming moon, but the moon in turn is caught in the tree of darkness, which many cultures believed to have its roots in the Underworld. While the moon was trapped in the massive tree, the sun would rise again to full strength.

The unicorn is not peculiar to the West. The Chinese also have a unicorn called Chin-Lin, one of the four animals of good omen, the others being the phoenix, dragon, and tortoise. The Oriental unicorn differs from the Western conception in that it has the body of a deer, the tail of an ox, and the hooves of a horse. Its horn is short and made of flesh, the opposite of the long, ivorylike horn of Western tradition. While according to some Western writers the unicorn is a fierce animal, the Oriental Chin-Lin is gentle in nature. So gentle that it walks softly on grass for fear of killing any other creatures.

When Confucius was born, Chin-Lin announced the birth to the philosopher's mother by spitting out a piece of jade that had written on it: "Son of the essence of water, kingdoms shall pass away, but you will be a king, though without a throne." Seventy years later the unicorn was caught and killed. Confucious went sorrowfully to see it and noticed it still wore the ribbon his mother had tied to it at birth.

Chin-Lin has been pushed into the background along with other Confucian myths by the Chinese communists, so the animal has not been subjected to any modern Chinese investigation. In the West, however, whether the unicorn existed or not has continually been of great concern to many scientists and lay believers. Up until the start of the French Revolution, in 1789, the unicorn's horn was still used to detect poison in royal dinners. Eventually scientific observation (or lack of it) won out, and the animal was declared a figment of the imagination. We do have the evidence of Dr. Franklin Dove, a biologist, who apparently tried to create his own unicorn. He wrote in 1933 that he had performed an operation on a one-day-old Ayrshire calf in which a single spike was solidly attached to its skull and could be used to pry up barriers.

Could such a beautiful and godlike beast then have really existed? Perhaps the truth is in Edward Topsell's remark in *Historie of Four-Footed Beastes*, written in the seventeenth century: "God himself must need be traduced, if there is no unicorn."

GORGONS, GERYON, ECHIDNA, HYDRA, MERMAID, MELUSINA, UNDINE, KRAKEN, AND LOCH NESS MONSTER

Medusa, the snake-haired monster, was once a very beautiful maiden, but she had the misfortune to be loved by Poseidon. The sea-god, like his brother Zeus, took what he liked, and he raped Medusa in the temple of Athene. That goddess, unable to punish one of her peers, struck with a vengeance at the girl and turned her into a monster with snakes for hair. Medusa had two sisters, Stheno and Euryale. Both sisters were immortal, Medusa was not.

In early Greek art the three, known as the Gorgons, were portrayed with protruding eyes and huge serrated teeth. If anyone gazed upon any of the Gorgons, the person would be turned to stone.

Perseus was sent by King Polydectes (who hoped the youth would not return) to fetch the head of the Gorgon Medusa. Athene helped him in his venture. The goddess gave Perseus a magic sword, winged sandals, a helmet that would make him invisible, and a mirror. At the opportune time Perseus turned his back to Medusa, looked into the mirror, and by wielding his sword backward, cut off her head. At the moment of her decapitation she gave birth to Poseidon's children, the winged-horse Pegasus and the monster Chrysaor. Chrysaor in turn became the father of Geryon and Echidna, two more monsters.

Geryon, a winged, triple-bodied creation, owned a herd of man-eating cattle guarded by Orthus, the two-headed dog. Heracles, in his Tenth

Labor, killed Geryon and the dog. Echidna, the other grandchild of Medusa, was half-woman, half-serpent, and gave birth to the Hydra of Lerna, yet another monster. The Hydra had a doglike appearance in some versions of the myth, but was generally more dragonlike in most accounts. It was said to have had as many as one hundred heads. As soon as one of the heads was cut off, two more would come up in its place. Some accounts say the heads were human; others, that they were serpentlike. Whatever— it is generally agreed that one of the heads was immortal. Spenser in *The Faerie Queene* settles for a mere seven heads:

> *Seven great heads out of his body grew,*
> *An iron breast, and back of scaly brass;*
> *And all imbued in blood his eyes did shine as glass,*
> *His tail was stretched out in wondrous length.*

The monster's breath would destroy all life, animal and vegetable, causing the place it inhabited to be a wasteland. The Second Labor of Heracles was to slay the Lernaean Hydra. The hero, not so dumb as he is often portrayed, called upon his friend Iolaus to burn each stump as soon as he cut off each one of the monster's heads. When Heracles was down to the last, the immortal head, he buried it under a great boulder, where it still seethes to this day, causing volcanic eruptions.

All these beasts descended from Medusa have made her a figure of great mythological fascination. Some say Medusa's head was given by Perseus to Athene. Freud, in one of his many short writings, says Medusa's head represents the female genitals, which men fear and are thus paralyzed by. Iris Murdoch uses this interpretation of the myth in her novel *A Severed Head*, in which the character of Honor Klein is Medusa-like in her ability to repel and immobilize. Medusa and her Gorgon sisters were sometimes shown in Greek art with a phallus attached to them, which according to Freud is a symbol of castration.

In modern Greek folklore Medusa and her sisters are half-woman, half-fish, who haunt the Black Sea on Saturday nights. This contemporary incarnation is related to the general European belief in mermaids, creatures half-fish, half-woman who have fascinated men for centuries. Mermaids are said to have gold or green hair and can be spotted on moonlit evenings, looking into a mirror as they comb their hair. Like the Sirens, their singing voices lure sailors to their deaths. Among their gifts is the ability to know the future. In the German epic poem of the Middle Ages, *The Nibelun-genlied*, Hagan, the slayer of Siegfried, captured the garments of two mermaids he found bathing in the Danube and forced them to reveal his future to him. They did: If he went to the land of the Huns, he would be killed. Hagan heeded their advice and did not take the journey.

Although they are only half-woman, men have fallen madly in love with mermaids in mythology and in the movies, too. In a 1940s movie, *Mr. Peabody and the Mermaid*, a very respectable businessman falls in love with a mermaid, and his staid life is never the same again.

Mermaids were sometimes baptized, as in the case of a mermaid in a sixteenth-century legend who was carried to the church in a vat. She was offered the choice of dying immediately after baptism and going straight to heaven, or of living some three hundred years and then receiving her reward. The mermaid chose the former and was baptized Murgen, or Sea Foam, and included in the calendar of saints.

Two other half-woman creatures connected with water are Melusina (who according to French legend was half-woman, half-serpent, and lived in a well) and Undine, a water sprite. Melusina was a woman most of the week, but on Saturday she had to return to her snake-fish form. She married Raymond, nephew of the Count of Poitiers, on the very modern-sounding condition that she be free on Saturday nights. One day her husband caught her in her snake-fish form and she had to flee. She left two children and is looked upon as the ancestress of three noble French houses. The central character in the story behind Mendelssohn's overture *The Fair Melusina* is based on her legend.

Undine, the water sprite, could become a mortal if she married a human being. Should her husband be unfaithful, however, she had to return to her home in the sea. In the numerous legends and plays about her, such as Jean Giraudoux's *Ondine*, the man is invariably unfaithful.

Our next to last fantastic water creature is the Kraken, a fabulous sea monster or sea snake. His legend seems to have originated during the Middle Ages with numerous seamen's accounts of monsters haunting the deep. In a later account written in the eighteenth century by a Danish bishop, the Kraken was said to be a mile and half wide, with tentacles that could capture ships and bring them down. One legend tells of a bishop who, returning by sea to his own country, spotted what he thought was an island. He went ashore and said Mass. When he returned to his ship, he saw that it was not an island at all, but a Kraken afloat.

As recently as 1933 in Scotland a Kraken-like monster was said to have been "seen" by a motorist driving along the shore of Loch Ness. The new apparition, dubbed the Loch Ness Monster, reportedly has been seen by many other people, making the area even more interesting to tourists.

Does the monster really exist? The question still causes debate in local Scottish taverns. For us, however, the Loch Ness monster points out that under the proper psychological and naturalistic conditions, even our science-oriented age can conjure up a beast that can hold its own against any monster from ancient mythology.

THE BEASTS OF EZEKIEL, DANIEL, AND THE FOUR EVANGELISTS

Ezekiel, a Hebrew prophet of the sixth century B.C., one hot day was sitting down by the river Chebar in Babylonia when suddenly the hand of Yahweh God was upon him. Ezekiel wrote (1:4–10 RSV):

> As I looked . . . a stormy wind came out of the north, and a great cloud, with brightness round about it, and fire flashing forth continually, and in the midst of the fire, as it were gleaming bronze.
> And from the midst of it came the likeness of four living creatures. And this was their appearance: they had the form of men, but each had four faces, and each of them had four wings. Their legs were straight, and the soles of their feet were like the sole of a calf's foot; and they sparkled like burnished bronze. Under their wings on their four sides they had human hands. And the four had their faces and their wings thus: their wings touched one another; they went every one straight forward, without turning as they went. As for the likeness of their faces, each had the face of a man in front; the four had the face of a lion on the right side, the four had the face of an ox on the left side, and the four had the face of an eagle at the back.

The prophet's vision then goes on in considerable detail to describe theophany, or the manifestation of a god. Here Yahweh appears surrounded by four beasts. Ezekiel never describes Yahweh but merely relates

196

St. John the Evangelist is likened to the
eagle in the figure of the four living
creatures.

St. Bede the Venerable

that he saw "the likeness of the glory" of Yahweh. The four beasts are described in detail, however, though interpretation of the imagery is quite confused. According to some commentators on the Bible text the four beasts symbolize four leading gods of the Babylonian pantheon. The human-faced beast is Nabu; the lion-faced, Nergal, god of the Underworld and plague; the bull-faced, Marduk, and the eagle-faced, Ninib, god of hunting. If this is the correct interpretation of the imagery, it was Ezekiel's way of indicating these foreign gods were servants of Yahweh. While the Babylonian gods were merely manifestations of the forces of nature, Yahweh was the creator and sustainer of nature.

Ezekiel's vision had a great impact on later Biblical writing even though no Jew was allowed to read the passages until he was forty years of age, since the rabbis considered the symbolism too complex for the untrained.

When the Book of Daniel was written, its author recalled some of the imagery of Ezekiel. Daniel saw a winged lion, a bear, a winged leopard, and a "terrible and dreadful" beast with ten horns (7:1–28). Most Bible commentators believe Daniel's beasts to represent various empires that destroyed one another in the ancient world. Babylonia is represented by the winged lion; the Medes by the bear; the Persians by the leopard; the Greeks by the ten-horned beast, which destroys all the others in the vision.

The use of visionary animals in the Bible did not end with the Book of Daniel, for the author of the Book of Revelation also saw a vision of four beasts surrounding the throne of God (4:6–8). The four creatures were a lion, an ox, an eagle, and one with the face of a man. John's vision had great influence on later Christian art. Numerous works show Christ enthroned with these four beasts who came to symbolize the Four Evangelists. Matthew is represented by the angel-man, since his narrative dwells on the human nature of Christ. Mark's symbol is a lion, since the animal was believed to be born dead and brought to life after three days. The choice of the lion, however, is somewhat inappropriate for Mark, since his gospel lacks the full Resurrection account. Most Bible scholars believe the original gospel ending was lost and another hand completed the narration. In the *Revised Standard Version* Mark's account ends with verse 8 of chapter

16. The footnote includes the rest of the gospel (9-20). Verse 19 gives the account of Christ's Ascension to heaven.

The ox came to symbolize Luke's account, since the animal was used in sacrifice and Luke's narration emphasizes the atonement made by Christ's suffering and death. The eagle was chosen to represent John because his gospel dwells on the divinity of Christ and eagles fly close to the sun, according to legend.

These symbolic explanations, all from Christian sources, come after the fact, however, since the animals' symbolism existed long before Christian writers tried to explain their meaning. But by the fourth century the four beasts and what they symbolized had been established in Christian iconography. The four beasts are seen in Graham Sutherland's mammoth design for behind the altar of Coventry's new cathedral in England, rebuilt after the Nazi bombs destroyed it. The design shows a majestic Christ, draped in white, with the four beasts surrounding his enthronement. Even today the four mysterious animals stir man's deepest emotional responses.

MINOTAUR, CENTAURS, SATYRS, AND FAUNS

Minos was in line for the kingship of Crete, but his claim was disputed. To insure his accession to the throne Minos prayed to the sea-god Poseidon to send a bull from the sea for him to sacrifice to the god. The god sent such a beautiful bull, white with a black spot between its horns. Minos decided not to sacrifice the bull and substituted another. Poseidon was angry and went to Aphrodite, goddess of sexual passion, to make Minos' wife Pasiphae fall in love with the beast. The king, upon learning of his wife's infatuation with the bull, ordered the artist Daedalus to devise some way to satisfy the queen's lust. (Minos seems to have been a very understanding husband.) So Daedalus built a hollow wood form, covered it with cowhide, and Pasiphae placed herself inside it. The bull, excited by the sight of what he thought was a cow, had intercourse with Pasiphae and from their union was born Asterius, the Minotaur, half-man, half-bull.

Minos now had the problem of what to do with the beast, and he again called on Daedalus. To house the Minotaur the artist constructed a labyrinth, a multiplex of courts and dead-end passages with continual mazes. With the beast safely out of the way, the king went about his usual business of making war and oppressing his people, as well as enjoying his wife as if nothing had happened.

Their son Angrogeus won the Panathenaic games but was waylaid and killed by some envious Athenians on his return journey. Minos marched on Athens and forced the city to pay a ransom for the death of his son.

Periodically, the city was to send seven youths and seven virgins to be sacrificed to the Minotaur. (The myth does not indicate what the Minotaur ate before this new diet was prescribed.) The Athenians delivered the payment twice, but on the third time around the lot fell to Theseus, son of Aegeus, king of Athens. Theseus was determined not to die as the others. He made his way to the court of King Minos. Ariadne, the daughter of the king, fell in love with Theseus and decided to help him combat the Minotaur. She gave Theseus a ball of thread to find his way out of the labyrinth. The Minotaur and Theseus met, and the young Athenian killed the monster. Using the ball of thread, he escaped with Ariadne. But the hero soon tired of the girl and abandoned her on the isle of Naxos.

Theseus had told his father that he would hoist white sails upon his return if the adventure were a success, black ones if it were a failure. Through some mistake, or perhaps through deliberate plotting on Theseus' part, black sails were raised. The king believed his son was dead and threw himself from a cliff into the sea, thus leaving the throne to Theseus. After many more adventures the killer of the Minotaur was murdered by another king.

The Greek myth of the Minotaur has influenced many artists and writers. James Joyce chooses the name of the artist Daedalus for the family name in his novel *Ulysses*. Picasso used the monster in a series of works in which the beast symbolizes the blind, savage nature in man. Yet, terrifying as the animal is, he often evokes some love or pity on the part of the viewer. One of Picasso's best evocations of the beast is found in his etching *Minotauromachia*.

Commentators on the Minotaur myth see the beast as a part of the bull-and-sun cult on Crete, similar to the Baal-Moloch cult of the Phoenicians, whose victims were destroyed by fire. The union of Pasiphae and the bull is seen as reflecting the sacred marriage between the Queen and the Bull-God during a religious festival. Athens also had a ritual in which its women were married to the bull-god Dionysus. Others see Theseus' slaying of the bull as a myth representing the end of human sacrifice, in the same way as some read the story of Isaac and Abraham in Genesis (chapter 22).

A beast half-animal, half-human seemed to appeal to the Greeks, for they also had in their mythology Centaurs, half-horse, half-man. Some commentators try to explain the origin of this union of the two as a misconception of the Greeks, who early in their history were unfamiliar with cavalry and saw the horse and rider as one. This theory finds support in Prescott's *History of the Conquest of Mexico*. The native Aztecs panicked when they saw a Spanish rider fall off his horse, since they believed the horse and man to be one and the same. The cool Roman poet Lucretius, in his magnificent work *De Rerum Natura,* or *On the Nature of Things,* states conclusively that the Centaur is an impossibility, since the horse would reach maturity before the man. The human part of the Centaur at three years of age would be a baby while the horse part would be full grown.

This reasoning, however, had little effect on mythology, which supplies more than one account of their birth. One legend says the Centaurs were the sons of Ixion, king of Lapithae, who was invited to dine with Zeus on Mount Olympus. Ixion, however, tried to seduce Zeus' wife Hera, but the god substituted a cloud for Hera. From this union of the cloud and Ixion the Centaurs were born. Zeus later punished Ixion by having him bound to a fiery wheel. Another myth says the Centaurs were the children of Apollo's son Centaurus and Silbia; another myth says they were the offspring of Centaurus and the mare of Magnesian.

The Greeks used Centaurs in their art and literature to represent barbaric civilization. One Greek myth captures this view. At the marriage feast of Pirithous and Hippodamia the principal Centaurs were invited. Previous to the wedding the Centaurs had never tasted wine and one of them, Eurythion, became so drunk that he tried to abduct the bride. A tremendous battle ensued in which the Centaurs were much the losers. Rubens brilliantly painted a version of the battle, and Ovid tells the tale with relish in his *Metamorphoses.*

Not all the Centaurs, however, were lascivious drunkards. The Centaur Chiron, son of Cronus and an Oceanid, was a friend to man, teaching him the arts of healing, hunting, and music. He was the tutor of Asklepius, the god of medicine, and the tutor of Jason, Achilles, and Heracles. During a fight with the Centaurs one of Heracles' poisoned arrows accidentally struck Chiron, who was immortal. In order to avoid suffering from a wound for eternity, Chiron asked Zeus to let him die instead. The god, out of pity, placed Chiron in the heavens as Sagittarius, the archer, the ninth sign of the Zodiac.

In Christian art the good qualities of Chiron were forgotten and the earlier mythological Centaur of lascivious appetites was emphasized. In

Sassetta's painting *St. Anthony Abbot with a Centaur,* the fourth-century saint is shown with a Centaur, whom the saint has obviously overcome and converted to sexual abstinence.

In Hindu mythology the Gandharva or Kinnara are half-animal creatures usually shown with a horse's body and a man's head. Hindus believed they were the spirits of slain warriors. From the half-horse, half-man concept it is a short step to the half-goat, half-man, or the Greek satyrs and Roman fauns. These creatures had pointed ears and hooked noses, and they were attendants of the god Dionysus. They danced, played reed pipes, and chased and raped nude nymphs in the woods. Countryfolk used to sacrifice lambs to them, as well as offering them the first fruits of the harvest.

Nathaniel Hawthorne, in his last complete novel *The Marble Faun,* considered the dual nature of the beast. Two Americans in Rome, Kenyon, a sculptor, and Hilda, a New England girl, met a mysterious woman, Miriam, whose past was somewhat unclear. The three became acquainted with Donatello, Count of Monte Beni, a handsome Italian who resembled the Faun of Praxiteles, an ancient statue, though his curly hair prevented their determining whether or not his ears were pointed. Donatello's nature, a blending of the human and the animal, resulted in an amoral attitude toward life, which led to both love and murder.

Hawthorne raises many questions in the novel concerning the dichotomy of animal-human personality. Kenyon says toward the end of the novel:

> *Sin has educated Donatello, and elevated him. Is Sin, then—which we deem such a dreadful blackness of the Universe—is it, like Sorrow, merely an element of human education, through which we struggle to a higher and purer state than we could otherwise have attained? Did Adam fall, that we might ultimately rise to a far loftier Paradise than his?*

This question is left unanswered by Hawthorne. Yet the question has plagued Judaism and Christianity for thousands of years. Was the Fall of Adam and Eve actually fortunate? Was the loss of innocence for the better? Perhaps the question will never find a satisfactory answer. But the symbols of the man-beast, whether Minotaur, Centaur, or Faun, indicate that the question of the balance of man's physical and spiritual makeup still lurks in his imagination.

PHOENIX, FENG-HWANG, HO-O, SIMURG, ROC, ANKA, AND FIREBIRD

Heiliogabalus, the third-century A.D. Roman Emperor, was noted for his sensual appetites. He devoted most of his time to either sexual or culinary pursuits. He was known particularly for his side dishes: pearls in his steamed rice, gold shavings in his peas, and various precious stones in other vegetables. He loved to eat bird brains, the tongues of peacocks, and flamingo heads. What he desired most of all, however, was the fabulous Phoenix, the marvelous bird of wonder that is said to have appeared only five times in all history.

All the lackeys of the emperor searched the known earth for the Phoenix. Many birds were sent for his inspection, but the emperor doubted the authenticity and credentials of them all. Finally one day a proconsul brought to Rome from a far island of the Eastern seas a bird that had never been seen at the court, and he stated that this was the Phoenix, the Bird of the Sun. (It was probably a Bird of Paradise.) The gluttonous Emperor had the bird prepared and ate it.

Herodotus, the historian, not so easily fooled as the Roman emperor, includes the tale of the Phoenix in his *Histories*, but confesses he does not believe in its existence. He writes:

I have never seen the Phoenix myself save in paintings, for it is exceedingly rare and visits the land of Egypt (as I was told at Heliopolis) only at intervals of five hundred years, upon the death of the parent bird. Its plumage, judging from paintings, is partly gold and partly red, while in shape and size it resembles the eagle. This is the story they relate of the Phoenix: it brings its parent all the way from Arabia enclosed in a lump of myrrh and buries the body in the Temple of the Sun. In order to do this it shapes a quantity of myrrh into the form of an egg as large as it can conveniently carry. It then hollows out the lump, places the parent bird inside, and covers the hole with more myrrh. That done, it carries the egg to the Temple of the Sun in Egypt.

The Greek historian's suspicion that there might be more myth to the Phoenix legend than truth is correct. The Phoenix legend probably originated as a sacred symbol of the sun at Heliopolis in Egypt, either as a stork, heron, or egret. The bird represented the sun, which died in its own fires every night and rose from them the next morning.

The imagery of the Phoenix rising from its own ashes appealed to the early Christians as a symbol of the Resurrection of Christ. St. Clement, a convert by St. Paul, refers to the Phoenix in one of his letters to attest to the truth of Christ's Resurrection. One reason cited for the omission of Clement's letter from the canon of the New Testament is his mention of the Phoenix, which some churchmen said did not exist at all. This, however, did not stop the medieval imagination. A twelfth-century Latin bestiary, translated by T. H. White, says:

If the phoenix has the power to die and rise again, why silly man are you scandalized at the word of God—who is the true one of God —when he says he came down from heaven for men and for our salvation, and who filled his wings with the odours of sweetness from the New and Old Testaments, and who offered himself on the Altar of the Cross to suffer for us and on the third day rise again?

The Christian adaptation of the symbolic Phoenix, however, had some warrant in Hebrew Scripture. The Book of Job (29:18) mentions the bird:

> *Then I said: "I shall die with my nest,*
> *And I shall multiply my days as the phoenix. . . ."*

This translation from the Jewish Publication Society's 1917 version differs from the standard rendering in the King James Version and from the *Revised Standard Version,* both of which substitute "sand" for "phoenix." Both words in the original Hebrew are similar and the matter is left to the translator, but it seems as if King James' men and the Reviser's panel chose "sand" to avoid any mythical connotation in the Bible verse. Certainly sand does not multiply!

While the king's translators may have been squeamish about naming the mythical beast in their version, he nevertheless thought the bird was an ideal image for monarchs—God's regents on earth, according to the now defunct belief in the divine right of kings. James I was not alone in his belief. Others, Queen Elizabeth I, Mary Queen of Scots, and Queen Jane Seymour all used the Phoenix for symbolic purposes on their arms, medals, and tokens.

Oriental mythology includes phoenixlike creatures in its tales and legends. The Feng-Hwang are male and female birds in Chinese mythology, symbolizing everlasting love. The Japanese Ho-o, another phoenixlike creature, came to earth to perform good deeds and thus help mankind. After each manifestation it reascended to heaven. In Persian mythology the Simurg, an immortal bird, was the connecting link between heaven and earth. It lived some seventeen hundred years and after its young were hatched, one parent burned itself to death. Arabic folklore, based in part on Persian mythology, developed the Roc or Rukh, a fabulous white bird of gigantic proportions that could lift elephants and carry them to its nest, where they would be eaten for dinner. One such bird is described in the tale of Sinbad in *A Thousand and One Nights.* The Anka, another Arabic creation, was made by Allah to eat the wild beasts of Palestine to make room for the Children of Israel. The bird, however, ate too much and thus left the land rather barren in parts.

The Oriental and Western Phoenix creations are blended in the Russian firebird of numerous folktales. This fantastic creature inspired the well-known *Firebird* ballet of Igor Stravinsky.

The Master said, "The Phoenix does not come; the
river gives forth no chart. It is all over with me."

Confucian Analects

The Phoenix, and all other phoenixlike creations in mythology and
legend, point out man's desire to transcend his finite existence by choosing
a symbol that expresses his hope of rebirth and resurrection. When news-
papers were reporting the rebuilding of Coventry Cathedral in England,
destroyed by Nazi bombers during the Second World War, the expression
that the cathedral rose "from the ashes, phoenixlike" was often used. Although the analogy might have been overdone in the popular press, the use
of the mythical bird again symbolized man's ever-determined spirit.

GRIFFIN, HIPPOGRIFF, PEGASUS, AND CHIMERA

Of all creatures the griffin—a monstrous half-eagle, half-lion—most loved gold and precious stones. He would roam the Caucasus Mountains in search of treasures, and when he found them, he would gather them together, sit and watch them for hours, fascinated by their gleam in sunlight and moonlight. Nearby dwelt the ugly one-eyed Arimaspians. They lived by a cave that was the home of the North Wind. These creatures worked the land, digging up gold and stones only to have them stolen by the griffin. The monster would hide until they had collected a large store, then, intercepting the sun's rays with his massive flapping wings, the griffin would swoop among the men. If his enormous claws grasped a man, they could crush him to death. Sometimes, very rarely, the Arimaspians were able to steal an egg or two of the griffin and in this way imposed some form of birth control on their unpleasant neighbor.

The griffin, often a sun symbol, drew the chariots of Zeus, Apollo, and Nemesis in Greek mythology; guarded the Gate to the Garden of Eden in the Bible (the cherubim were griffinlike creatures with a bull's body instead of a lion's); were one of the symbols of the evil Egyptian god Set; and were among the followers of the water-demon Tiamat in Babylonian mythology.

During the Middle Ages one of the numerous legends about the griffin concerned the magical properties inherent in its claws. So-called griffin claws, usually antelope horns, were made into drinking cups in the belief that they would change color in the presence of poison. Poisoning was common during the Middle Ages. Brunswick Cathedral had a griffin's claw brought from the Holy Land. It was placed on the main altar on certain feast days. Later legend said only a holy man could gain the claw in payment for curing the griffin of illness.

The symbolism of the griffin is unusually confused in folklore. In an Italian medieval bestiary the griffin stands for the devil, but St. Isidore of Seville, writing in his *Etymologies*, says: "Christ is a lion because he reigns and has great strength. He is also an eagle, because after his Resurrection, he ascended to Heaven." The griffin, combining the natures of lion and eagle, then fulfills the function of a symbol of Christ. This is the way many commentators on Dante's *Divine Comedy* see the vision of the griffin in Canto 29 of the Purgatory. Still others see Dante's griffin as a symbol of the papacy. The eagle part of the beast represents the pope as he is borne aloft to the throne of God to receive commands. The lion nature characterizes his kingship when he walks the earth.

This confusion is compounded by other writers who say that only the female griffin has wings—the male has spikes. Most artists, however, do not follow this point.

Winged or not, the griffin obviously had some family life. He fathered the Hippogriff, a fantastic beast half-horse, half-griffin, according to Ariosto's Renaissance epic poem *Orlando Furioso,* or *Crazy Orlando*. Ariosto says the animal is not his own invention, but really existed. Sired by a griffin, the Hippogriff's mother was a mare. The beast had his father's feathers (which we know only the female was said to possess), wings, forelegs, head, and beak—but the rest was all horse. The beast belonged at first to the enchanter Atlantes, but later came into the possession of Rogero. This hero, with the help of a magic bridle on the beast, traveled widely— England, Ireland, Ethiopia—finally going to the moon, where he found crazy Orlando's wits, or mind, in a bottle and brought them back to the distraught hero.

Ariosto's imagination had been stirred by the *Aeneid,* in which Virgil uses the poetic image to "cross griffins with horses" to signify something impossible. Ariosto knew his Greek as well as Roman mythology, and his horse's wings descend from Pegasus, the winged horse of Greek mythology that sprang from the blood of the decapitated Gorgon Medusa.

Pegasus was the offspring of Poseidon and was presented to the goddess Athene by her muses. The magic winged horse was captured by Bellerophon, also a son of the sea-god, who used the horse in his fight with the Chimera, the monster born of Typhon and Echidna, having a lion's head, the body of a goat, and the tail of a serpent or dragon. Flames flickered from the Chimera's mouth as it devastated the countryside of Asia Minor. Bellerophon destroyed the monster by raising himself on his winged horse Pegasus and shooting the beast with his arrows.

In one source the Chimera's origin is ascribed to a mountain in Lycia with a volcano at its top, goat pasture on its sides, and a base infested with serpents. Plutarch, however, rejects this fanciful creation and says Chimera was the name of a pirate captain who had the images of a lion, goat, and snake carved on his ship. Plutarch's explanation, however, is an attempt to avoid any mythological connotations in the animal's meaning by striving to explain its origin on a purely rational basis.

Whatever the true origin of the Chimera, Bellerophon, made proud by defeating the creature and envious of the gods, tried to ride his magnificent Pegasus to heaven. Zeus sent a gadfly, which stung the horse, causing him to fling Bellerophon from his back. The hero fell to the earth. The massive fall did not kill him but lamed him. He then made his way from city to city but no one befriended him, since that would offend the gods, whom Bellerophon had insulted with his pride. When he died, no one marked the time or place of his death.

SPHINX, HARPIES, SIRENS, SCYLLA, LAMIAE, AND EMPUSAE

Hera or Hades sent the sphinx to Thebes to punish the city for some offenses. The monster, daughter of Echidna by Orthus or Thyphon, had the head of a woman, the body of a lion, the tail of a serpent, and the wings of an eagle. It sat on a rock on Mount Phicium and would ask a riddle of all the young men who passed by. Those who did not answer the riddle correctly were devoured by the sphinx. Since the area surrounding the beast was covered with the decaying bodies of young men, the number of correct answers were few indeed.

One day Oedipus, the son of Jocasta and Laius, was on the road to Thebes when he was confronted by the sphinx. She looked at the handsome young man, a potential victim, and posed the riddle.

"What is it that goes on four legs in the morning, two at midday, and three in the evening," she said with a smile.

Oedipus looked up at her and replied, also with a smile: "Man. He crawls in infancy, walks upright in his prime, and leans on a cane in his old age."

The sphinx became so angry at the quick answer from the youth that she hurled herself from the rock, forgetting to fly, and fell to her death. Oedipus was then greeted as a hero and made the king of Thebes.

Pausanias, the Greek writer and traveler of the second century A.D., writes in his *Description of Greece* that the sphinx was a lady bandit who waylaid travelers, her headquarters being on Mount Phicium. Jung, however, in his interpretation of the encounter of Oedipus and the sphinx, says the creature represents the Great Mother-Goddess who is destroyed by the stronger masculine force, represented by Oedipus.

This Jungian interpretation finds support in the Babylonian version of the sphinx, in which it is a symbol of the moon-goddess Astarte, a Mother-Goddess. In the Egyptian version the sphinx is always male and often symbolizes royal strength and dignity. The Great Sphinx at Gizeh represents the god Horus trying to catch sight of his father Ra, the rising sun, as he journeys across the valley.

Emperor Augustus used on his seal the device of a sphinx with a man's face, bird's wings, and lion's paws. When he was in Asia the Roman Senators found his choice of a seal very appropriate because they thought most of his messages to them were riddles. The emperor later changed the device to that of Alexander the Great's portrait. In the end vanity won out, and he had his own image put on his seal.

While the sphinx had some dignity in its form, the harpies were foul-smelling creatures with the head and breasts of a woman, and the body and limbs of a vulture. They were three in number: Ocypeta, or Rapid, Celeno, or Blackness, and Aello, or Storm. Their claws were bronzelike and their wings metallic. They were afraid of metal objects, but they were fearless in their cruelty. The gods punished King Phineus for revealing the future by sending the harpies to torment him. The harpies would eat his food, leaving him very little—and that little covered with their waste. When the heroes of the Argo arrived, two of them went after the harpies as they attacked the king's dinner. But Iris, the rainbow goddess, came down from heaven and cried after the heroes, who had nearly destroyed the monsters with their weapons:

"It's not ordained that you should destroy the harpies. They are the hounds of mighty Zeus. I will swear they shall no longer attack you if you put down your swords."

The men listened to the goddess and the harpies left, angry but not willing to battle the metal weapons of the two Argonauts. This encounter is recounted in the epic poem *The Argonautica*, or *The Voyage of the Argo*, by Appolonius of Rhodes, a Greek poet who lived in the second century B.C., as well as in William Morris' long narrative poem *The Life and Death of Jason* written in the nineteenth century.

Harpy, from the Greek word *harpazein*, means to snatch or carry away, indicating that the harpies were originally wind-goddesses like Maruts in Hindu mythology, who wields golden weapons and lightning. Shakespeare in *The Tempest* (III.3) gives the stage direction: "Thunder and lightning. Enter Ariel, like a harpy; claps his wings upon the table; and with a quaint device the banquet vanishes." From this one would assume Shakespeare knew the original meaning of the harpies as well as the tale of the Argonauts' encounter with the creatures.

The half-bird, half-woman body of the harpies was similar to the Sirens in Greek mythology, though later art often pictured Sirens as beautiful women, draping the rocks and enticing sailors to their doom. When the crew of the Argo passed by them at the Strait of Messina, the entire crew would have been destroyed had Orpheus not played a lyre, drowning out with his music the song of the Sirens. When Odysseus passed by the same strait, he had his men fill their ears with beeswax to shut out the singing. He had himself tied to the mast so he could not jump into the sea at the sound of their voices. So Odysseus and his crew safely passed the test.

In the *Odyssey* only two Sirens are mentioned, but in later mythology there are three, Parthenope, Leucosia, and Ligeia. The Sirens' song inspired the last movement of Debussy's *Nocturnes for Orchestra*, which combines the sounds of the orchestra with a wordless female chorus, capturing the compelling mystery of the fateful calls.

Aside from the Sirens, the Strait of Messina had a female monster, Scylla, who would devour sailors passing through the strait. She was once a beautiful virgin but did not want to marry. When a sea-god, Glaucus, fell in love with her, Circe, who loved Glaucus, turned the beautiful girl into a monster. In one account she had a woman's head and six dogs for feet, in another telling she had six heads. In either case the girl found a lair on the promontory in the Strait of Messina, opposite the whirlpool Charybdis. Scylla would lean out to try to snatch sailors and bring them to their doom. Often if she did not succeed in her murder plan the whirlpool Charybdis would do away with the men.

Scylla and Charybdis have become proverbial in literature to denote opposite dangers that beset one's course. Virgil penned the line often quoted:

He runs on Scylla, wishing to avoid Charybdis.

The next mythological creation in this group of monsters with women's heads and animal bodies is the lamia, or, if you are unlucky enough to meet with more than one, lamiae. These were lascivious evil spirits in the form of a serpent with a woman's head, though they could assume human shape for a time and beguile men.

Lamia was one of the many loves of the great god Zeus. Naturally Hera was jealous as she was of all her husband's paramours. In a rage Hera killed the children Lamia had by Zeus. The distraught mother then vowed vengeance on all children. She was connected with demons called empusae, children of the goddess Hecate, who seduced young men and sucked their blood while they slept.

Goethe's poem "The Bride of Corinth" is based on the legend of a young man who marries an empusa who then sucks his blood by night. The lamiae, however, supplied Keats with the framework for one of his most fantastic narrative poems, *Lamia.* The story was taken by Keats from Burton's *The Anatomy of Melancholy*, written in the seventeenth century.

In Keats' version of the legend, Lamia, a witch, was transformed by the god Hermes from a serpent into a beautiful maiden. Lycius, a young man, fell in love with her and she in turn with him. The two were happy for a short time until the meddlesome philosopher Apollonius told Lycius that she was a serpent-witch. With a frightful scream she vanished, and Lycius died the same night.

Obviously the lamia legend holds some interest in Pop culture for it appeared in a Hollywood B movie, *The Cult of the Cobra* (1955), which told of a woman who turned into a snake to do away with a group of young men who had accidentally spied one of the cult's religious ceremonies. Despite some rather stiff acting and awkward dialogue the terror and fear still came through, only showing the force of the old myth.

DRAGONS

The gods Odin and Loki had to make payment to Hreidmar for killing Hreidmar's son Otter when they were out hunting. Hreidmar demanded gold, and the gods went to the dwarf Andvari, the guardian of a gold treasure and a magic ring. They stole the gold, but as they were escaping with it, the dwarf cried out that their loot would bring only ruin to everyone who touched it.

Odin and Loki paid no attention to the dwarf and rode off with the treasure. They filled an otter skin with the gold and set it before Hreidmar. However, they had left one muzzle hair still showing and Hreidmar demanded that it too be covered with gold. Odin drew the gold ring from his finger and placed it on the hair.

The dwarf's curse soon came true. Fafnir and Regin, sons of Hreidmar, killed their father and took the treasure. Fafnir loved the gold so much that he transformed himself into a dragon to guard the treasure all the better. Fafnir was content for some time until Sigurd, the great Northern hero called Siegfried in Wagner's *Ring of the Nibelung,* went out to kill the monster, encouraged by Regin.

Sigurd first dug a pit for Fafnir to fall into, but Odin, disguised as an old man, advised him to dig three pits instead of one.

"Sit in one pit, so you can put your sword through Fafnir's heart when he passes over. The other pits will catch his blood."

But there was the ancient Fafnir, and the Face of Terror lay
On the huddled folds of the Serpent, that were black and ashen-gray....

William Morris: *Sigurd the Volsung*

Sigurd made the pits as he was instructed. Now Fafnir came down to his watering place, and the whole earth shook about him as he snorted forth venom. Sigurd was not afraid of the dragon but sat waiting in one of the pits. When Fafnir crept over it, Sigurd thrust his sword under the left shoulder, and it sank in up to the hilt. Sigurd then jumped from the pit and thrust his arm up to the shoulder into the wound. The dying Fafnir asked Sigurd why he did such a horrible deed, and the youth responded with a very, very long answer.

After this monumental conversation Fafnir died, and Sigurd cut out his heart with his sword and roasted it. When the blood began to bubble out, Sigurd accidentally laid his finger in it and touched his mouth. Immediately he could understand the language of the birds. "Watch out!" a woodpecker warned him. "Fafnir's brother Regin, who goaded you on to kill the monster, will now kill you for his brother's gold. Remember he helped Fafnir kill their father Hreidmar." Without ado, Sigurd went to Regin and struck off his head.

This tale from the Icelandic *Volsunga Saga* has two motifs common to Western European dragon legends: a dragon who guards a treasure, and a hero who slays the dragon. After Sigurd slew Fafnir, he washed himself with the dragon's blood in one of the pits, which made Sigurd invulnerable except for one spot where a leaf stuck to his body. Later Sigurd was killed by Hagan, who discovered his vulnerable spot.

The gold brings a curse to all who touch it. G. B. Shaw, in *The Perfect Wagnerite,* sees the whole as a struggle between capitalists and workers and turns Wagner's *Ring* into a nineteenth-century socialist treatise. Shaw contends that his theory works for three of the music dramas, *Das Rheingold, Die Walküre,* and *Siegfried.* He feels, however, that *Götterdämmerung* does not fulfill the promise of these, since it descends into mere operatic melodrama, avoiding the social and political implications of the others.

Shaw's theory, however, has much more validity than the standard nineteenth-century interpretation of the legend, which says Siegfried's conquest of Fafnir was the freeing of the sun (symbolized by the gold) from night (symbolized by the dragon).

Often, however, the hero not only slays the dragon, he also frees a girl. Jung, in writing about such legends, sees the hero's conquest of the dragon as symbolic of the hero's *anima*, the part of his personality that is woman. Thus the killing of the dragon is the hero's coming into full manhood, since he casts off his female counterpart.

Because the dragon makes a rather comical sight to most twentieth-century eyes, some Jungians view the locomotive as its modern equivalent. The standard old movie plot of the girl tied to the railroad tracks with the oncoming, steam-belching iron engine who is freed by the handsome cowboy now serves as the symbol of the hero-dragon-maiden legend.

Christian symbolism is far less complex than Jung regarding the dragon's role. The mythical animal is simply the devil, according to the Book of Revelation (20:1–2). The Christian devil derives from the dragon in the Old Testament, descended, as we have seen earlier, from Tiamet, the Babylonian female dragon-monster.

Since the dragon is the devil in Christian symboilsm, numerous saints' lives depict the combat between the two forces. St. Philip, one of the apostles, destroyed a huge dragon that hid in the shrine of the god Mars. St. Michael, mentioned in the Book of Revelation (12:7), combats the devil-dragon, and St. Margarite is often shown with a dragon.

Margarite was the daughter of a pagan priest in Antioch during the reign of the Emperor Diocletian. The governor of the city wanted to marry her. But Margarite was unwilling to marry a pagan. In fact she did not want to marry at all but preferred to remain a virgin. The governor, so upset by her decision that he lost his reason, had the girl locked up in a dungeon. During the night the devil appeared to her in the form of a dragon. She was not in the least disturbed. She simply raised her cross and the beast fled in the night.

Another version of the legend says that the dragon swallowed the recalcitrant Margarite, but the cross she always wore grew to such proportions inside the dragon that he was split open and the saint saved. In both versions of the legend the governor had the saint executed in the end.

We have not forgotten the most famous of all dragon slayers, St. George. The feast of this popular figure has been kept in England on April 23 since the thirteenth century, and he has been the patron saint of that country since the fourteenth. Scholars and churchmen have argued who George was —if he was at all. Gibbon, author of *Decline and Fall of the Roman Empire*, writes that George was an Arian Bishop of Alexandria. Others say George was a Roman officer martyred near Lydda during the Diocletian persecution. St. Bede, taking a middle course, says George was beheaded, though most of the tales are "numbered among the apocryphal writings."

The legend of St. George may just be a Christian reworking of the Greek myth of Bellerophon and the Chimera. Certainly the ancients had their quota of mythological dragons. In Egyptian mythology Horus, in combat against Set (symbolized by a crocodile), slew the demon. In Greek mythology Thyphon, the son of Thyphoeus the Earth, was a hundred-headed part-human dragon. One of his hands reached to the west, the other to the east. From the hips down he was shaped like two wrestling serpents, and he was taller than a mountain.

Zeus, fearing that Thyphon would destroy the gods, sent a lightning bolt from far away to destroy the monster. Then from closer range Zeus struck Thyphon with a steel sickle, pursuing the beast to Mount Kasion. With the monster wounded, Zeus went even closer, but was caught in the coils of the dragon, who cut the sinews from Zeus' hands and feet. Thyphon then took Zeus to a cave called Leather Sack, where he hid the sinews of the god in a bear's pelt. He set Delphyne, a female dragon half-woman, half-serpent, to guard Zeus. Hermes and Aigipan, however, came to the rescue of Zeus. They stole the sinews and gave them back to Zeus, who took up his pursuit of Thyphon, this time in a chariot drawn by winged horses. At Mount Nysa the dragon was betrayed by Fate, who offered him some fruit to restore his strength, but the fruit was named "Only for a Day." Zeus followed Thyphon till they reached Sicily, where he hurled Mount Etna on the beast. The volcano still spits forth the fire of the dragon.

A smaller version of the mythological dragon with serpentlike qualities is the basilisk, from the Greek meaning "little king," or cockatrice, another name for the basilisk, said to be born from the yokeless egg of an old cock. (In Basil in the fifteenth century an old cock was tried for having laid such an egg. Found guilty, the bird was executed for the crime.) The basilisk, hatched by a toad on a dunghill, was called the king of all serpents, and its face was so ugly it could kill with one look. In Shakespeare's *Romeo and Juliet* (III.2) we have:

> *Say thou but "I,"*
> *And that bare vowel "I" shall poison more*
> *Than the death-darting eye of cockatrice.*

To avoid being killed by the cockatrice medieval Europeans would carry a mirror so the animal upon seeing itself would be killed instead. Sometimes travelers would carry with them a cock or a weasel, two mortal enemies of the cockatrice, to fight the beast.

In all of Western mythology it is difficult to find a kind word about the dragon. Perhaps the only exception is the fairy tale *The Reluctant Dragon* by Kenneth Grahame, which tells of a dragon that did not want to fight the knight at all.

Although the West is obsessed with the dragon as evil, the East sees the mythical beast as a beneficent animal. In China the emperor's throne was referred to as the Dragon's Throne and his face, the Dragon's Face. At the emperor's death it was said he ascended to heaven like the dragon. As a dragon ascends to heaven, the pressure of its feet on the clouds causes rain; thus the identification of the dragon with rain and watery places in Oriental mythology. Dragons often live in marshes and rivers and have kingdoms undersea, sometimes coming to land as Dragon-Kings in human shape.

Lung Wang is the Chinese dragon-king and supernatural rainmaker. His followers rise to the skies, dive into the water, and can achieve any shape they please. In Chinese mythology dragons controlled storms and were often associated with water spirits. (Gargoyle comes from *La Gargouille,* the legend of a dragon that lived in the Seine, ravaged Rouen, and was finally killed by St. Romanus, seventh-century Bishop of Rouen.)

Storms result when dragons are angry. One thing they particularly dislike is impoliteness. They also like to eat certain delicacies such as sparrows. It is advisable that your breath not smell of sparrows as you cross a bridge, for surely a dragon will come up and devour you.

Although they are sometimes capricious, they are also wise. In Chinese mythology dragon-horse was a messenger of heaven who "revealed" Yin and Yang, the two forces of the universe, to the Yellow Emperor. The Yin or Female is passive, dark, even numbers, and cold; the Yang or Male principle is growth, light, activity, heat, and odd numbers. Yin is often symbolized by valleys and women; Yang by men, sky, mountains, pillars, and the dragon. Also, in the *I Ching* the dragon symbolizes Wisdom.

One of the most common motifs in Chinese art is that of the dragon with its claws outstretched, reaching for a disk. Some explain the disk as the sun that the dragon tries to swallow—a watery creature; it wishes to drown the heat of the day. Others see the disk as a pearl or the moon.

Regardless of the explanation, the dragon holds a high place in Chinese mythology. It appears as one of the four great constellations in Chinese astronomy, and the new year is celebrated on the appearance of the moon before the rising of the dragon-star.

In the beginning of things men were as animals and animals as men.

American Indian

EPILOGUE

Should there be any moral in this book (and here we go back to medieval bestiaries), it is that no animal is good or bad, proud or humble, chaste or lecherous, except in man's imagination. Animals fill their role in the world in conformity with nature, not with man's subjective judgments. No animal has yet written a book to give us his or her view of the species Homo sapiens.

How *would* man fare in an animal's estimate?

ANNOTATED BIBLIOGRAPHY

My intention has been not to burden the reader with footnotes or a bibliography citing the hundreds of books and articles consulted and read for *Zoo of the Gods*. I have instead compiled a shorter annotated bibliography of some of the sources should the reader wish to refer to them. Since many other book titles appear in the text, they are repeated here only when the additional information may be of help to the reader. .

The most comprehensive book on animal mythology is still the two-volume nineteenth-century work *Zoological Mythology or The Legends of Animals* by Angelo De Gubernatis (Trubner & Co.; London, 1872; reprinted by Singing Tree Press, Chicago, 1968). The work contains a wealth of information as well as summaries of myths, fables, and legends relating to animals. The writing style, however, is dull and often confusing. A major drawback to the book's scholarship is its insistence on ascribing nearly every incident in mythology to a natural phenomenon such as Dawn, Sunset, Wind, Storm, or the like.

More recent books on animal lore and legend are *Fabulous Beasts* by Peter Lum (Pantheon Books, New York, 1951) and *Unnatural History* by Colin Clair (Abelard-Shuman, London, 1967). For a strictly medieval viewpoint of various animals *The Bestiary* translated by T. H. White (Capricorn Books, G. P. Putman's Sons, New York, 1960) provides a translation of a twelfth-century Latin bestiary, which is not only fun in itself, but White's notes make the book even more interesting.

Two books are useful for information on birds, *The Folklore of Birds* by Edward A. Armstrong (Dover Publications, New York, 1970 edition) and *Birds in Legend, Fable and Folklore* by Ernest Ingersoll (Longmans, Green and Company, New York, 1923; reissued by Singing Tree Press, Chicago, 1968).

Sir James George Frazer's *The Golden Bough* edited by Theodor H. Gaster in a new one-volume abridgment of the massive work (Criterion Books, New York, 1959) under the title *The New Golden Bough* is both must reading and fascinating. Frazer's work greatly influenced English literature in the early part of the century as well as various schools of psychology. Gaster corrects many misinterpretations of Frazer in this new edition and adds additional notes to help bring the text up to date.

Of encyclopedias dealing with mythology the thirteen-volume *Mythology of All Races* edited by Louis Herbert (Cooper Square Publishers, New York, 1964 edition) has a volume for each "major" mythology. The writing as well as the information varies considerably in each volume. Max Muller's volume on Egyptian mythology displays a scorn for many of the myths. When he translates one Egyptian text dealing with masturbation, he puts the "offensive" lines into Latin. In fairness to Muller, his text was written early in the century when such "editing" was necessary.

The best book on Egyptian mythology remains *The Gods of the Egyptians: Studies in Egyptian Mythology* by E. A. Wallis Budge (The Open Court Publishing Company, Chicago, 1904; reissued by Dover Publications, New York, 1969).

Funk & Wagnalls Standard Dictionary of Folklore, Mythology and Legend edited by Maria Leach (Funk & Wagnalls, New York, 1950) is generally quite good and up-to-date. The classic thirteen-volume *Encyclopaedia of Religion and Ethics* edited by James Hastings (Charles Scribner's Sons, New York, 1908–21) is dated. The article on "Animals" by Northcote W. Thomas does, however, have some interesting remarks on the roles of various animals in mythology and folklore.

Aside from the King James Version of the Bible, which is the version quoted in the text unless otherwise specified, various modern translations are helpful, such as *The Jerusalem Bible,* the *Revised Standard Version,* and *The New English Bible. The Analytical Concordance to the Bible* by Robert Young, for the King James Version, is a classic work containing thousands of English references, with Hebrew and Greek words. Various reprints are available.

Books about the Bible are endless; here are some of the more important reference works. The monumental twelve-volume *The Interpreter's Bible* (Abingdon Press, Nashville, 1952) is wonderful reading and also quite enlightening when checking Biblical references. The companion four-volume *The Interpreter's Dictionary of the Bible* (Abingdon Press, Nashville, 1962) is the most complete Bible dictionary. *The Jerome Biblical Commentary* edited by Raymond E. Brown (Prentice–Hall, Englewood Cliffs, N.J., 1968) offers a modern Catholic viewpoint of Biblical texts. Selected Biblical texts are covered in *Myth, Legend, and Custom in the Old Testament* by Theodor H. Gaster (Harper & Row, New York, 1969). The book uses comparative mythology to explore the texts.

The legends built around Biblical subjects are found in *The Lore of the Old Testament* and *The Lore of the New Testament,* both by Joseph Gaer (Grosset & Dunlap, New York, 1966), and in *Legends of the Bible* by Louis Ginzberg (The Jewish Publication Society of America, Philadelphia, 1966). The Gaer volumes give sources for the legends at the back of the book. The Ginzberg volume, however, does not, since it is a one-volume abridgment of a much longer work. A handy volume of those legends not contained in the New Testament canon are found in *The Apocryphal New Testament* translated by Montague Rhodes James (Oxford University Press, London, 1924). One major draw-back is that the translator's English style unsuccessfully tries to recapture the majesty of the King James Version.

A book covering Christian and Jewish lore in relation to other mythologies is *Curious Myths of the Middle Ages* by Sabine Baring-Gould (Longmans, Green and Company, New York, 1901 edition; reissued by University Books, New York, 1967). Baring-Gould was one of those gifted scholars who could write brilliantly.

The best book on Christian symbolism remains *Sacred and Legendary Art* by Anna B. Jameson (various editions), written in the last century. The volume contains a wealth of information on nearly all aspects of Christian symbols, with particular attention to the lives of the saints. There is also an earlier work, *Butler's Lives of the Saints* (various editions). Butler tends, however, to be rather stiff and awkward in his tellings, but he does give many of the legends, though often accepting them at face value. The *Lives of the Saints* by Sabine Baring-Gould (J. Hodges, London, 1872–77) is the most comprehensive work available to the English reader.

Of the never-ending books on Greek and Roman mythology *The Greek Myths* by Robert Graves (Penguin Books, Baltimore, 1955) is wonderful reading, whether one agrees or disagrees with Graves' controversial theories. *Myths of the Greeks and Romans* by Michael Grant (A Mentor Book, New American Library, New York, 1962) gives a comprehensive view of the subject with particular emphasis on the arts and various schools of psychology. *The Gods of the Greeks* by Carl Keréni (Penguin Books, Baltimore, 1958) offers a Jungian interpretation and is quite interesting, even if one does not accept, as in the case of Graves, all the conclusions.

The mythology of India is complex and confusing to the Western reader, since so many of its concepts are alien to Western thought. *Myths of the Hindus and Buddhists* by Ananda K. Coomaraswamy and Sister Nivedita (George G. Harrap & Company, New York, 1913; reissued by Dover Publications, New York, 1967) retells the myths and legends for the Western reader. The book, however, does not contain an index to facilitate its use. The volume on the mythology of India in *Mythology of All Races*, cited earlier, is useful, as is the volume on the mythology of China in the same set. There are two good collections of Chinese tales: *The Golden Casket: Chinese Novellas of Two Millennia* translated by Christopher Levenson from Wolfgang Bauer's and Herbert Franke's German version of the original Chinese (George Allen and Unwin, London, 1965); *Folktales of China* edited by Wolfram Eberhard (The University of Chicago, London, 1965.)

Northern mythology is covered in the four-volume *Teutonic Mythology* by Jacob Grimm (George Bell and Sons, 1883–1888; reissued by Dover Publications, New York, 1966). Grimm's work has none of the charm of the better known household tales, or fairy tales, he compiled with his brother, but he does cover his subject thoroughly. *Scandinavian Mythology* by H. R. Ellis Davidson (Paul Hamlyn, London, 1969) and Davidson's *Gods and Myths of Northern Europe* (Penguin Books, Baltimore, 1964) are two well-written, fascinating studies of a complex subject that still causes debate among many scholars. An earlier book, the volume on Eddic mythology in the *Mythology of All Races* set, also is of some interest but is by no means as well written as the Davidson studies.

If Northern mythology causes dissension among scholars, Celtic mythology is an even more difficult subject to organize. *Celtic Mythology* by Proinsias MacCana (Paul Hamlyn, London, 1970), though containing some interesting photographs, assumes too much knowledge of Celtic mythology on the part of the reader. It is, however, a comprehensive survey of the subject. *Irish Folk Stories and Fairy Tales* edited by William Butler Yeats (published 1888; various reprints available) and *Celtic Fairy Tales* edited by Joseph Jacobs (various reprints available) contain a wealth of tales that are interesting reading in themselves. Some scholars, however, object to Jacobs' volume on the grounds that he "overedited" the tales and thereby destroyed their more "primitive" quality.

English folktales appear in *Folktales of England* edited by K. M. Briggs and R. L. Tongue (The University of Chicago Press, London, 1965), a more scholarly collection than the well-known *English Fairy Tales* and *More English Fairy Tales* edited by Joseph Jacobs and published in the last century (various editions and reprints available).

Three books supply useful information on South and Central American mythology: *Mexican and Central American Mythology* by Irene Nicholson (Paul Hamlyn, London, 1967); *South American Mythology* by Harold Osborne (Paul Hamlyn, London, 1968); *The Gods of Mexico* by C. A. Burland (Eyre & Spottiswoode, London, 1967).

For North American mythology of both the native Indians and the European settlers the following are quite good: *American Indian Tales and Legends* by Vladimir Hulpach (Paul Hamlyn, London, 1965); *The Indians' Book: Songs and Legends of the American Indians* recorded and edited by Natalie Curtis (Dover Publications, New York, 1968); *North American Indian Mythology* by Cottie Burland (Paul Hamlyn, London,

1965); *A Treasury of American Folklore* edited by B. A. Botkin (Crown Publishers, New York, 1944).

The best collection of Italian folktales is the classic *Il Pentamerone* by Giovanni Batiste Basile (various English translations available). Also of interest is *Italian Fables* by Italo Calvino (The Orion Press, New York, 1956). It is a pity, however, that the massive folklore of Italy, combining as it does both pagan and Christian lore, is not available as yet in any English language book.

The rich folklore of Russia is found in *Russian Fairy Tales* translated by Norbert Guterman (Pantheon Books, New York, 1945) and in *Myths and Folk-Tales of the Russians, Western Slavs, and Magyars* by Jeremiah Curtin (Little Brown and Company, Boston, 1890).

African tales and folklore are available in *African Mythology* by Geoffrey Parrinder (Paul Hamlyn, London, 1967) and *Myths and Legends of Africa* by Margaret Carey (Paul Hamlyn, London, 1970). These books are particularly valuable for the reader not familiar with the vast mythology and lore of this massive continent.

INDEX

Compiled by Gary Gabriel Gisondi

The following index is in three sections:

I. General index to the animal lore of *Zoo of the Gods,* including the principal mythological and historical personages mentioned throughout the work.

II. Index to the authors, composers, painters, film-makers (and other artists) whose work or thought is mentioned in the text.

III. Index to works of multiple or anonymous authorship cited in the text.

Note: **Boldface** page numbers indicate principal treatment of subject.

I. GENERAL INDEX